The Cursive Lettered Snake

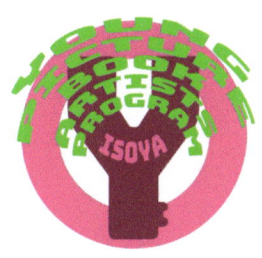

Young Picture Book Artists Program

Young Picture Book Artists Program

FOREWORD

The International Society of Young Artists (ISOYA) is a non-profit organization affiliated with the Losget Academy, founded in 2019 in Los Angeles. In 2019, ISOYA initiated the "Vibrant Future" International Education Project for Young Artists — a project dedicated to the artistic education of young people. In less than 4 years, the project has led to the publication of 9 individual art portfolio books and the collective artbook "International Artist Artwork Series". The project has also helped many ISOYA members enter top-ranked art schools and universities worldwide.

In 2021, ISOYA initiated the Young Picture Book Artists Program, which aims to provide guidance for young artists who are interested in creating picture books. The program has resulted in several published picture books, short films and related products.

The Cursive Lettered Snake is the third published picture book launched by the Young Picture Book Artists Program and is also Elaine V. Kuang's second published picture book after A Dream. Elaine is an outstanding member of ISOYA and holds great skills and talent in art. More importantly, she always puts all her efforts into the processes of creating these fabulous pieces. The Cursive Lettered Snake can be used to educate young children and help them discover the fun in cursive letters. With a very well established and creative idea, this book holds a great social practical value and coincidentally demonstrates Elaine's ability to serve the community with her artistic abilities — it is truly gratifying for a 15-year-old. By assisting the creation of these picture books, ISOYA aims to contribute to the children and young adult books market, and to set positive examples for young picture book enthusiasts.

ISOYA welcomes all aspiring young artists and art enthusiasts to join our organization. It is our mission to discover and cultivate the artistic potential in young people, and we sincerely hope that every art lover has the opportunity to receive the artistic education they desire. As a non-profit organization, we greatly appreciate the support and donation from the public.

May the artistic seed in every young artist sprout into flourishing blossoms. Nourished by the rich soil of education and moistened by the cool dew of inspiration, they shall produce the sweetest nectar of art.

Mark Harris
August 29, 2022

Mark Harris
President of the International Society of Young Artists
Adviser of the Young Picture Book Artists Program
Author of the art series East 100

Young Picture Book Artists Program

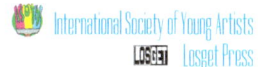
International Society of Young Artists
Losget Press

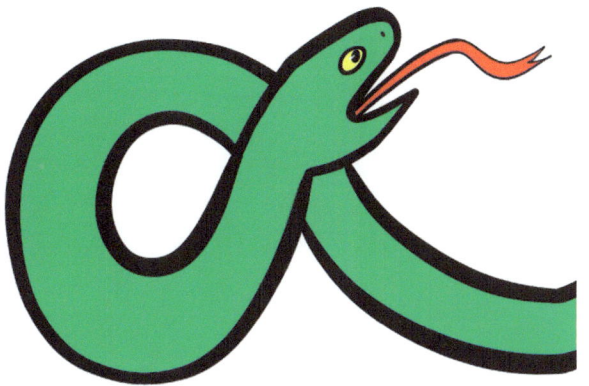

THE CURSIVE LETTERED SNAKE

Author: Elaine V. Kuang
Adviser: Mark Harris
Editor-in-Chief: Mark Harris
Editors: Elaine V. Kuang, Xinping Luan
Cover designer: Elaine V. Kuang
Book designer: Elaine V. Kuang
Photographer: Elaine V. Kuang

Author: Elaine V. Kuang
Adviser: Mark Harris
Editor-in-Chief: Mark Harris
Editors: Elaine V. Kuang, Xinping Luan
Cover designer: Elaine V. Kuang
Book designer: Elaine V. Kuang

Copyright © 2022 by International Society of Young Artists
All rights reserved.
Published in the United States by Losget Press, Los Angeles.
Originally published in paperback in the United States by Losget Press, in 2022.
Library of Congress Cataloging-in-Publication Data
Names: Kuang, Elaine V., author.
Title: The Cursive Lettered Snake/ Elaine V. Kuang.
Description: First edition. | Los Angeles: Losget Press, 2022.
Identifiers: LCCN: 2022916438/ ISBN: 978-1-951364-36-6
www.isoya.org
E-mail: isoya2018@gmail.com
First printing. 2022.

PREFACE

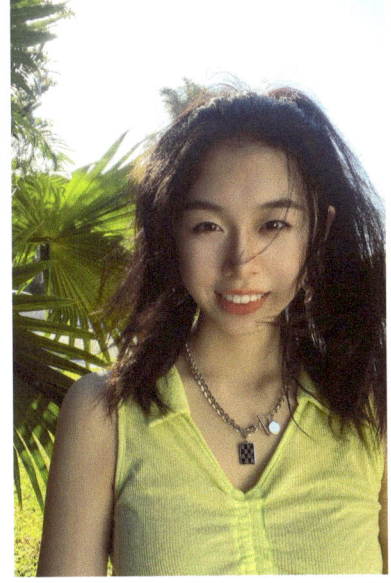

Elaine V. Kuang selfie in Los Angeles in 2022.

This is the second picture book I created at 15 years old. The process of making picture books is something that makes me feel extremely happy and elated—it fascinates me. Unlike novels, picture books are infused with both literature and art which allows my creativity to burst into both realms. I can satisfy my passion for writing and feel the joy of illustrating at the same time. I sincerely appreciate the guidance my mentor Mr. Mark Harris has provided me with. Without him I wouldn't have discovered my passion and talent in art.

These pieces implement the use of a cartoon animal to help children develop an interest in writing cursive. I hope this book can play a role in helping them discover the fun in learning. Whether it's those who have just started learning cursive or those who do not know cursive at all, this book will be beneficial.

I decided to express the letters in the form of animals since they are more lively and interesting for children to look at. The reason why I chose to base the book on a snake, rather than any other animal is because of the snake's shape. Though there are some other limbless animals similar to the snake, like earthworms, snakes have appeared more in fairy tales so children should be more familiar with them.

When creating the appearance of the cartoon figure, I needed to make sure that it looked both like a snake and a cursive letter. Despite having practiced cursive for numerous years, the process was challenging. Some letters like "i" and "x" have lines in which they are separated and are not easily arranged by the snake's body. This created some complexity for me, but after experimenting with different methods, I decided to use branches and leaves to supplement the incomplete shapes. Sure enough, the results were ideal. I ultimately chose green for the snake because the color of nature creates a more lively and harmonious vibe for the book.

I hope that the green snake can be the children's first stepping stone into taking interest in cursive. May this book guide you on the learning journey with cursive.

Elaine Kuang
Aug 30, 2022

Young Picture Book Artists Program

The Cursive Lettered Snake

abcdefghijklmnopqrstuvwxyz

A fun cartoonish way to raise children's interest and familiarity with cursive.

Young Picture Book Artists Program

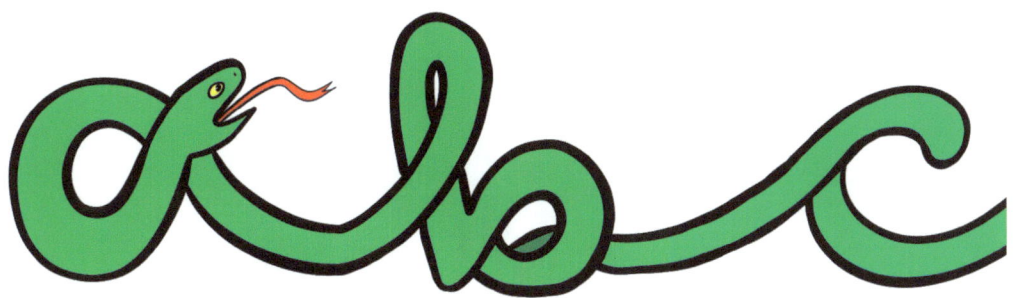

THE CURSIVE LETTERED SNAKE

Young Picture Book Artists Program

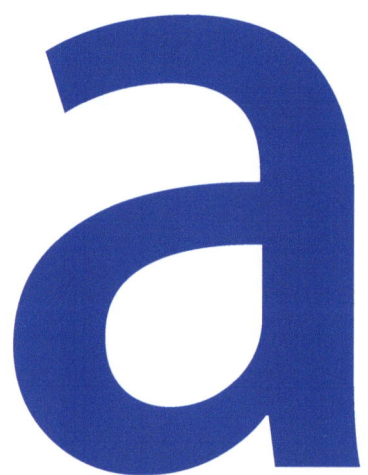

The Cursive Lettered Snake

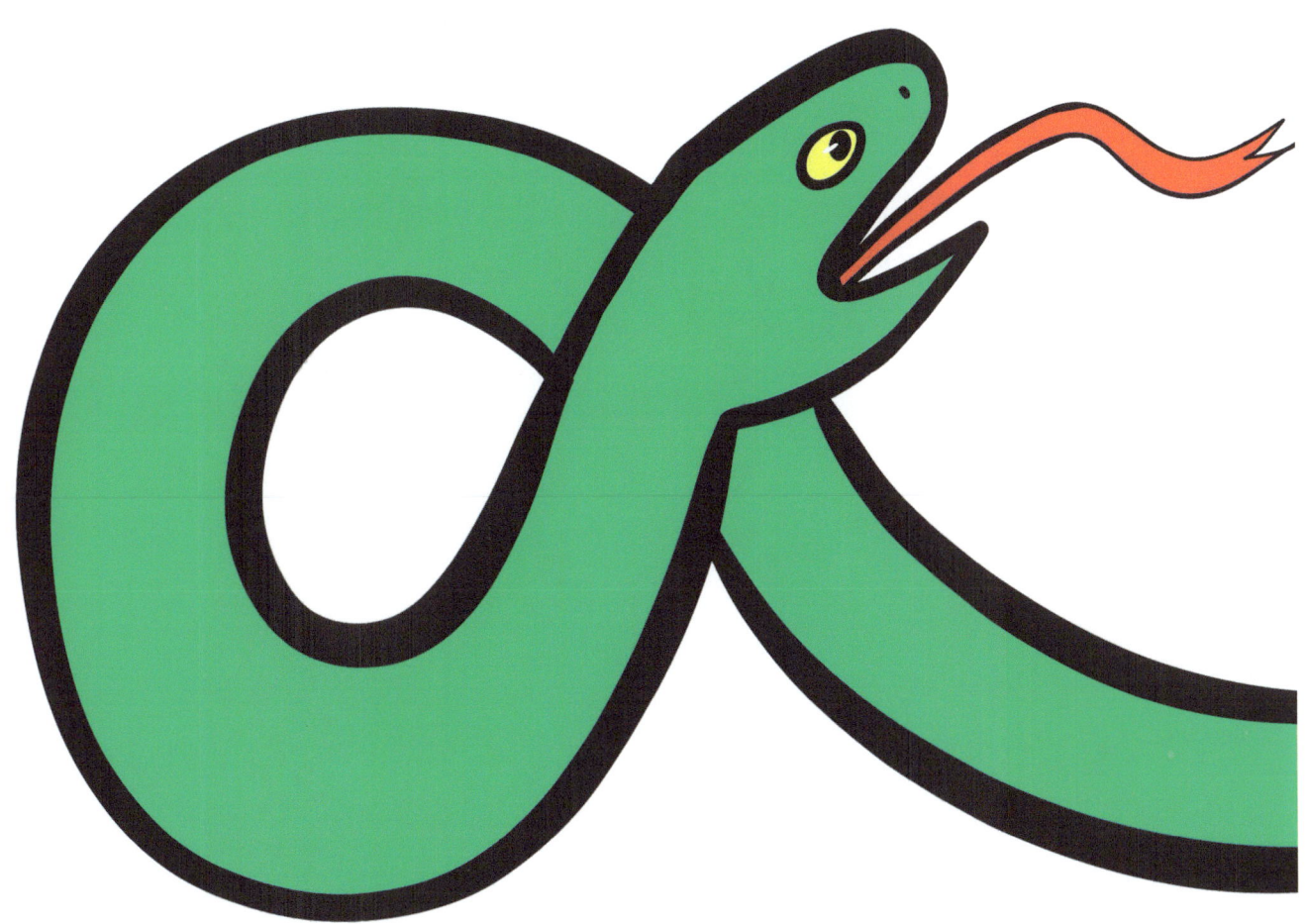

Young Picture Book Artists Program

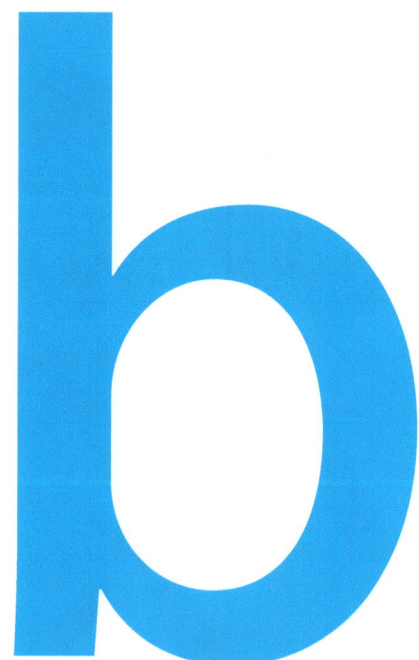

The Cursive Lettered Snake

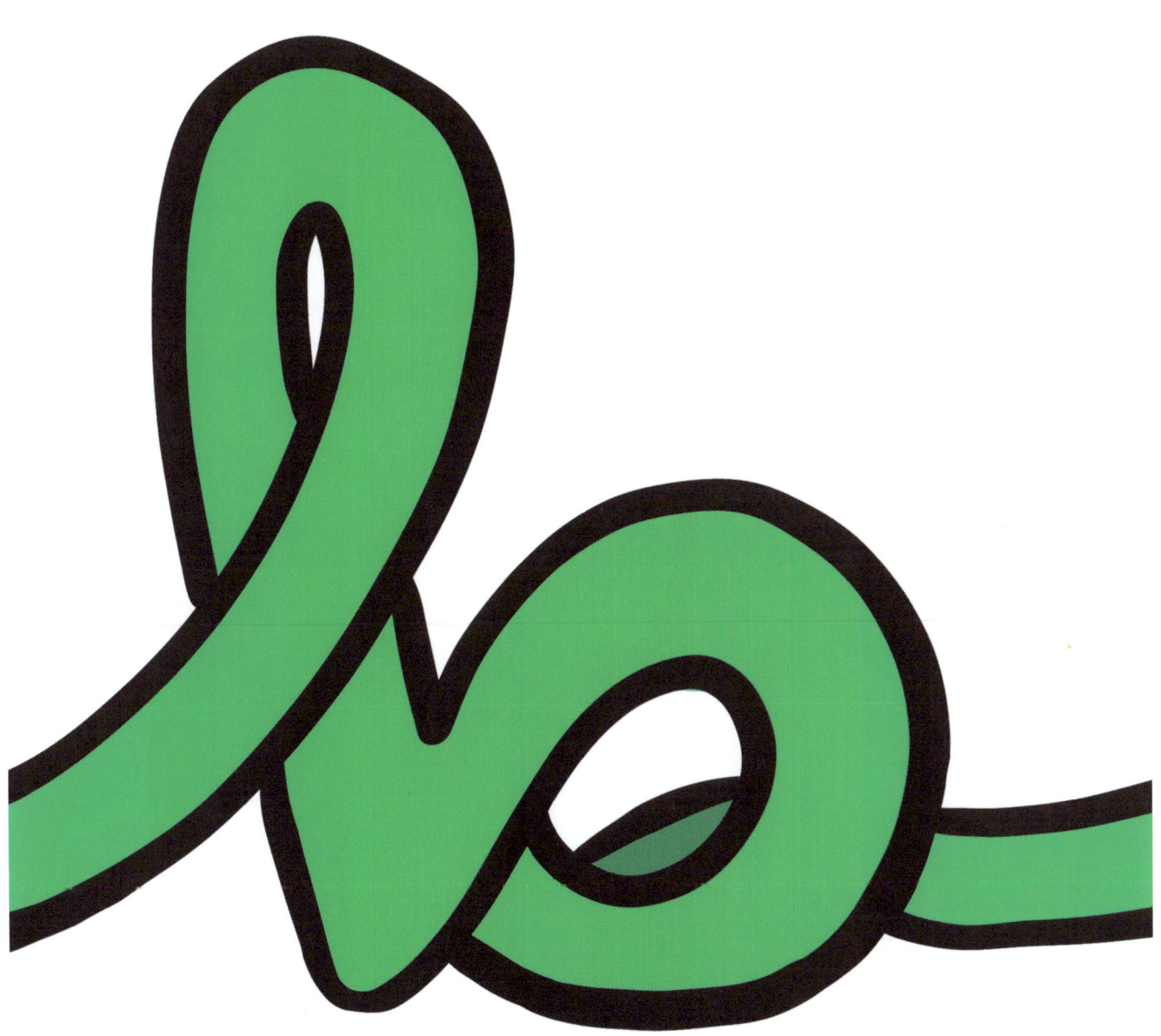

Young Picture Book Artists Program

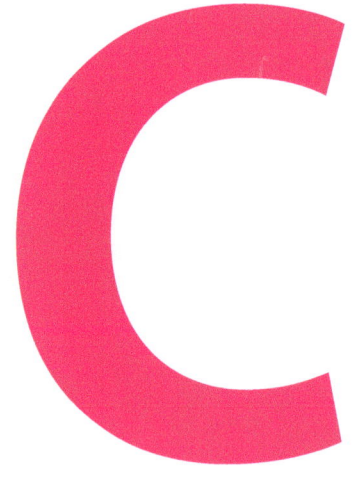

The Cursive Lettered Snake

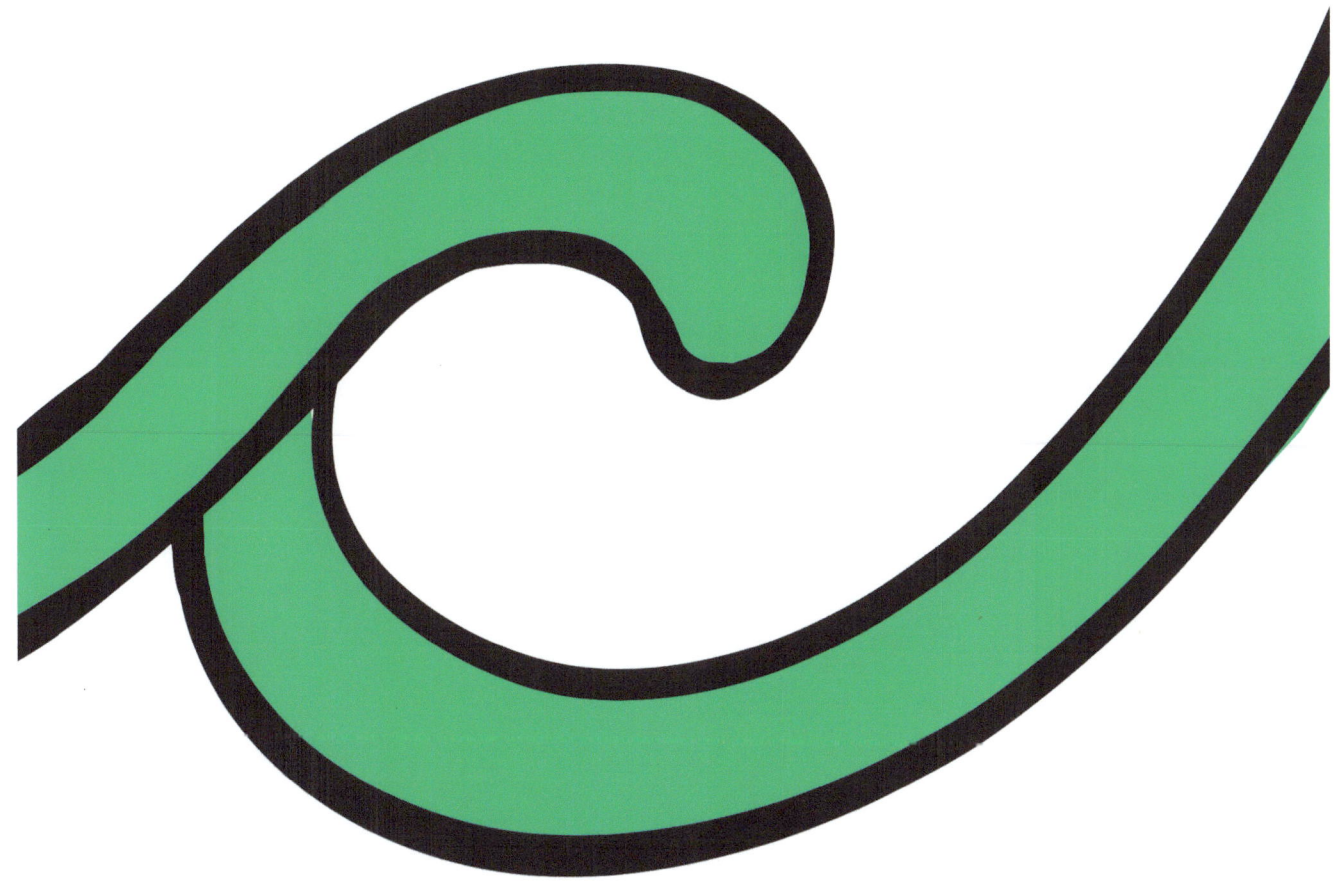

Young Picture Book Artists Program

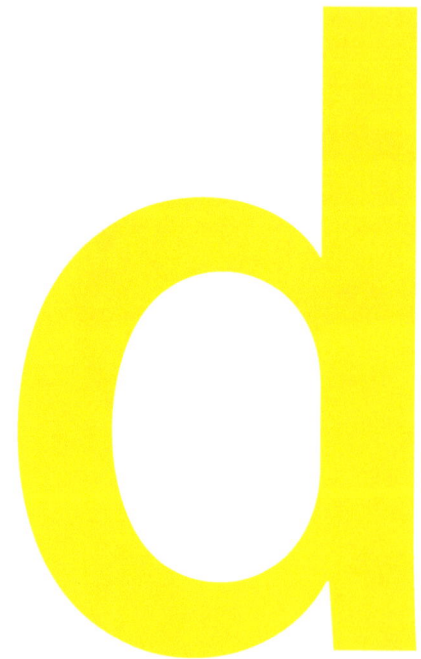

The Cursive Lettered Snake

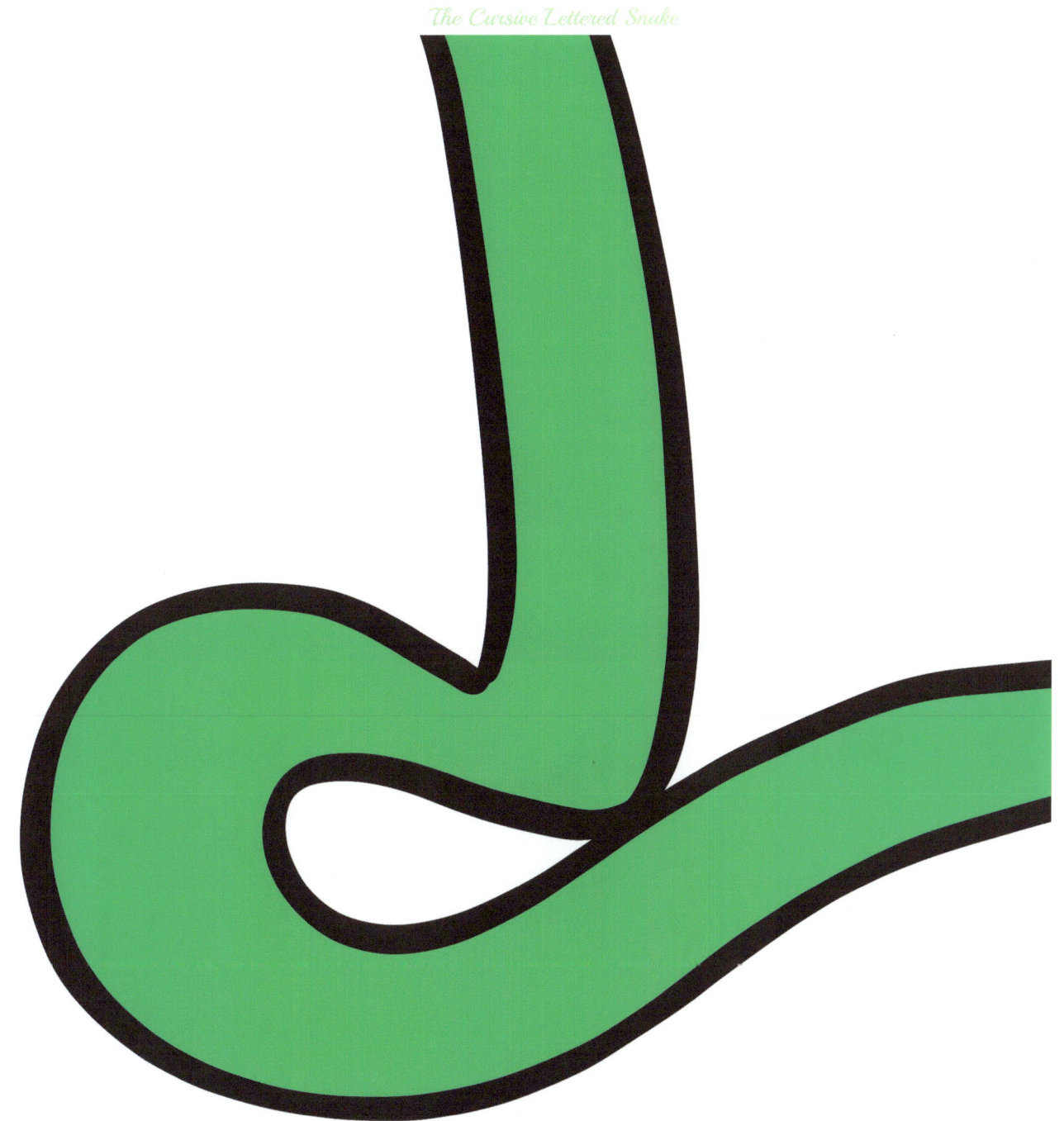

Young Picture Book Artists Program

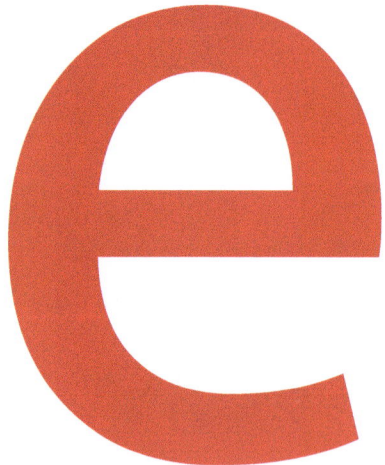

The Cursive Lettered Snake

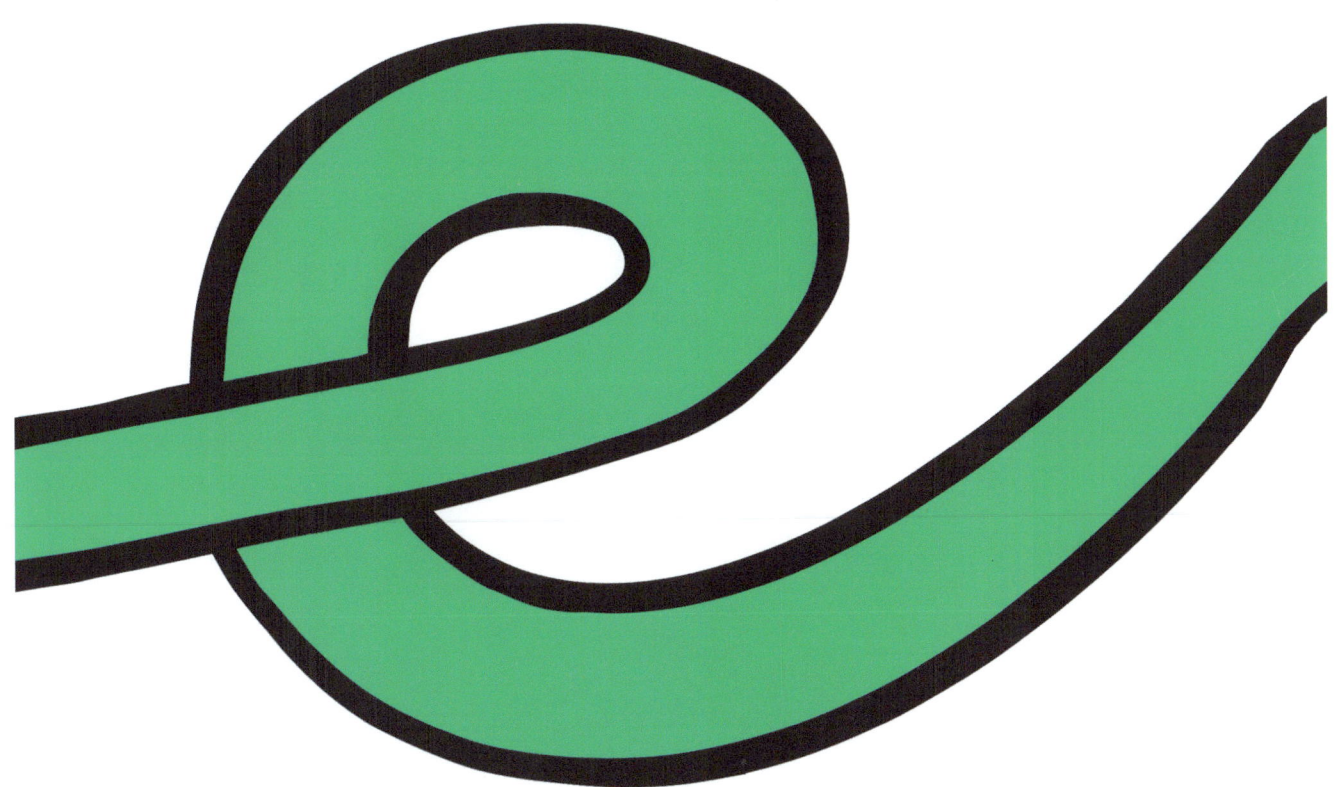

Young Picture Book Artists Program

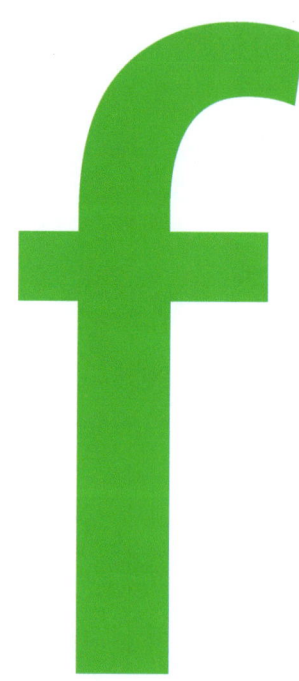

Young Picture Book Artists Program

The Cursive Lettered Snake

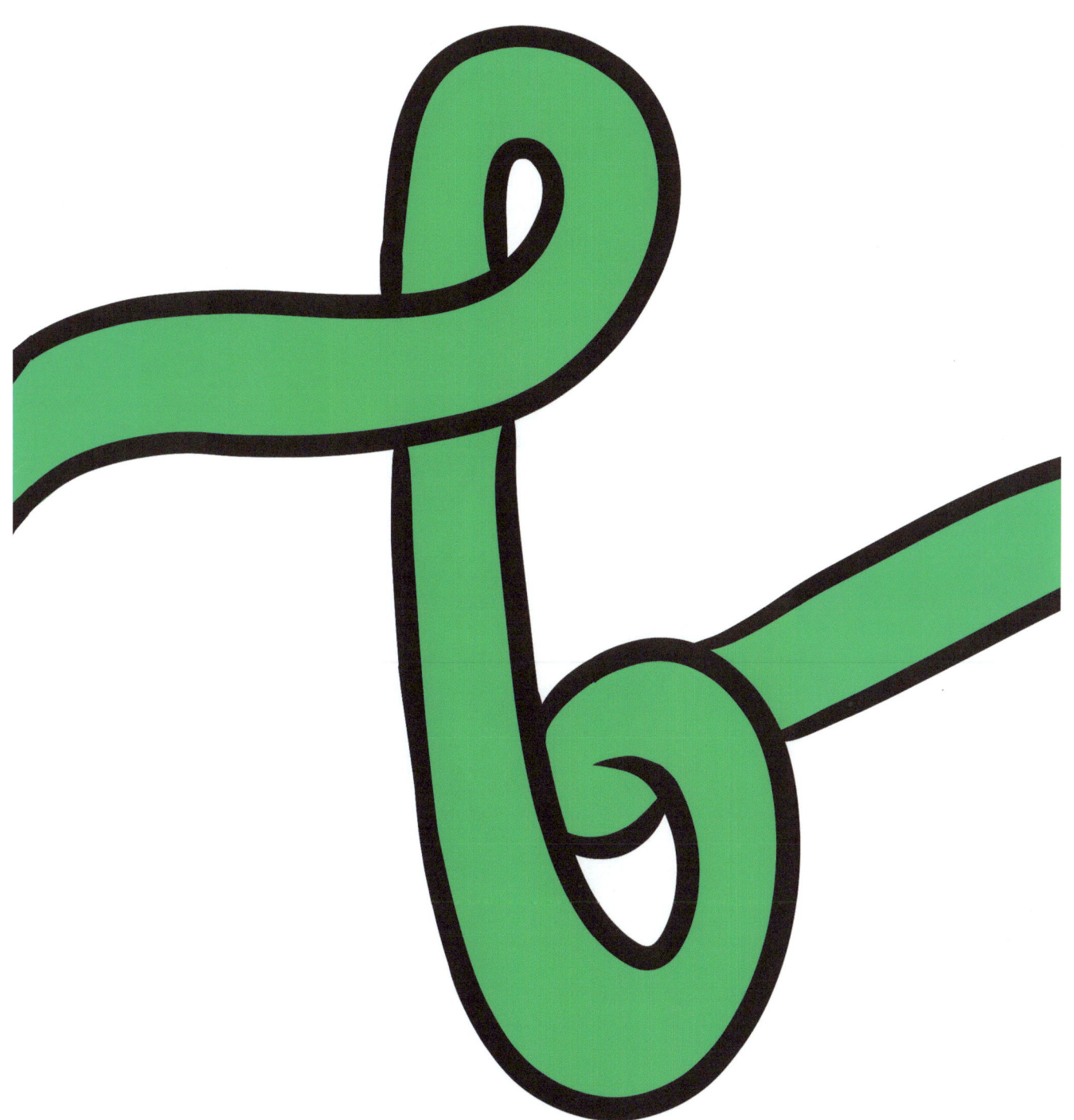

Young Picture Book Artists Program

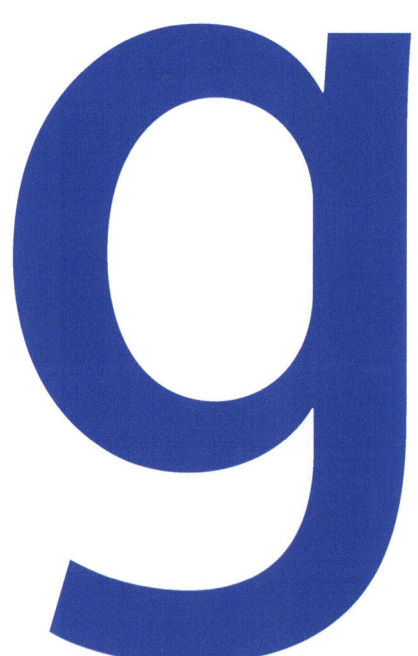

The Cursive Lettered Snake

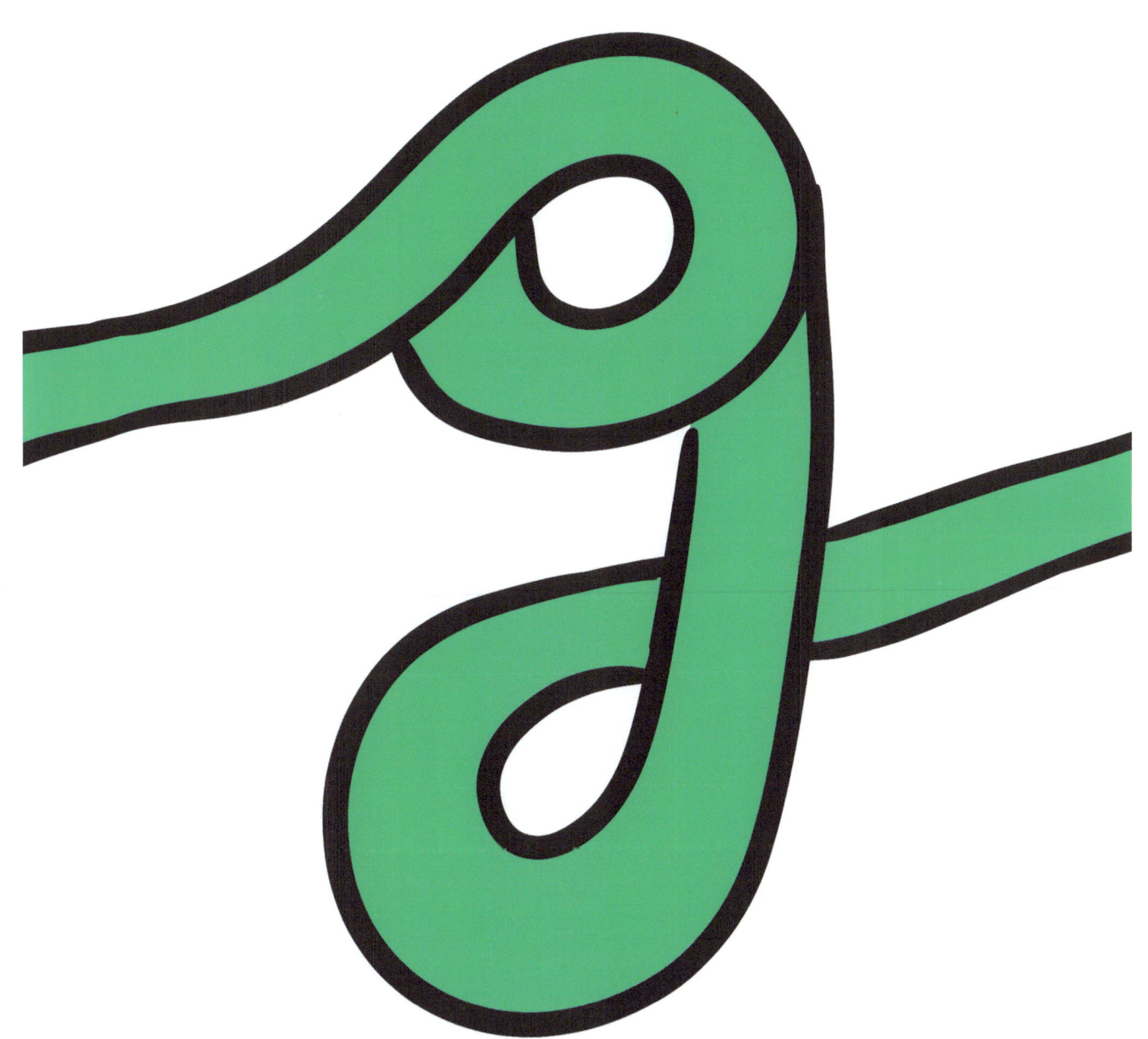

Young Picture Book Artists Program

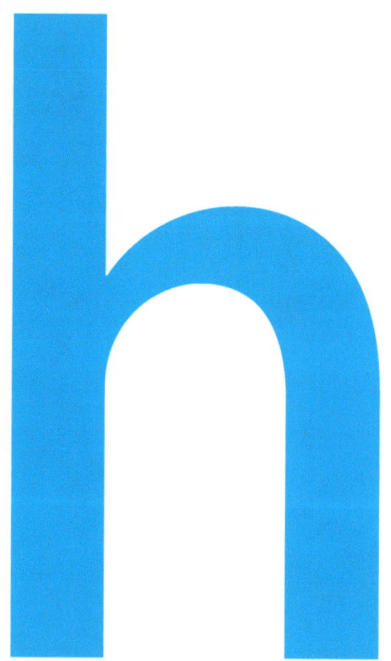

The Cursive Lettered Snake

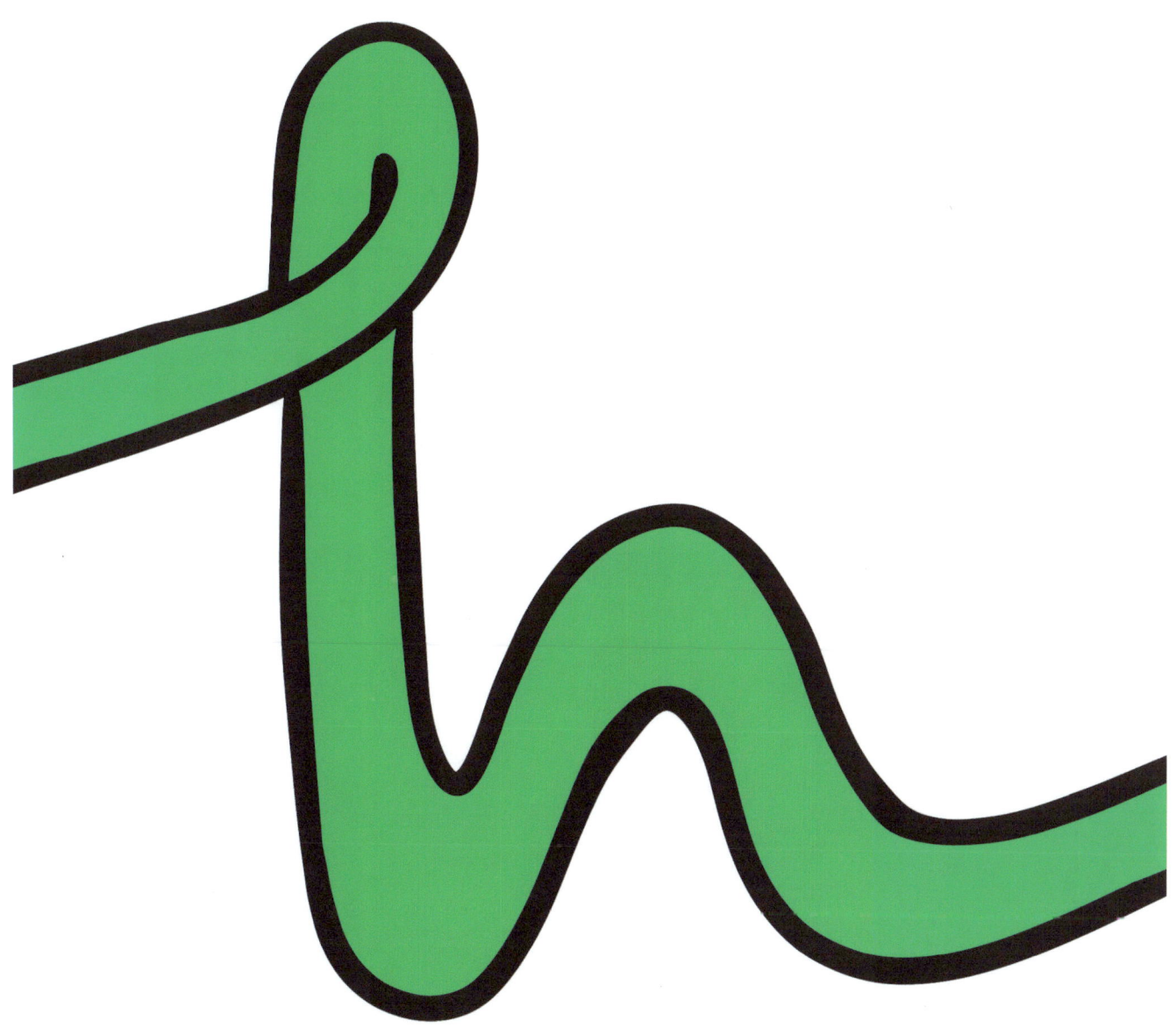

Young Picture Book Artists Program

The Cursive Lettered Snake

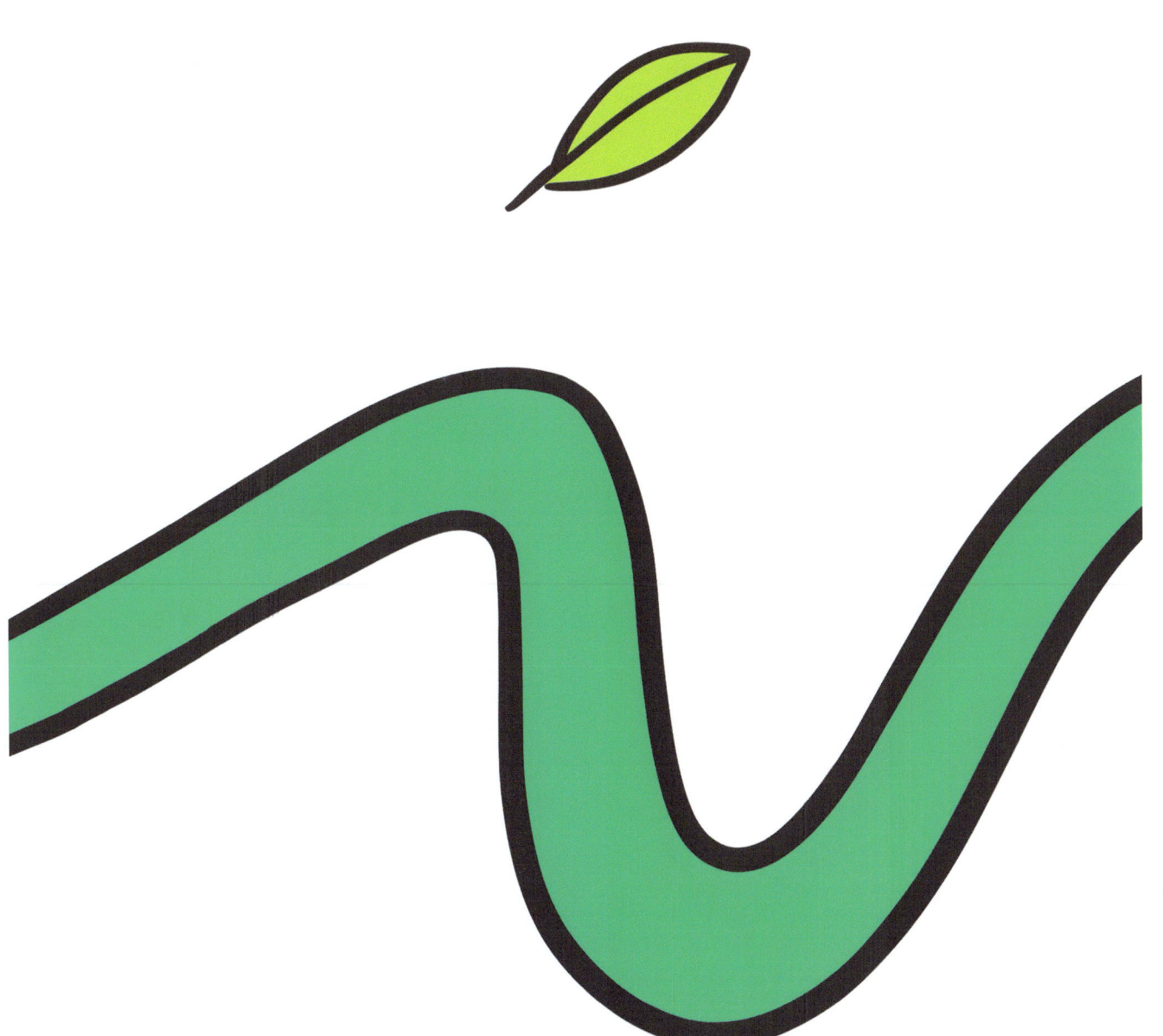

Young Picture Book Artists Program

The Cursive Lettered Snake

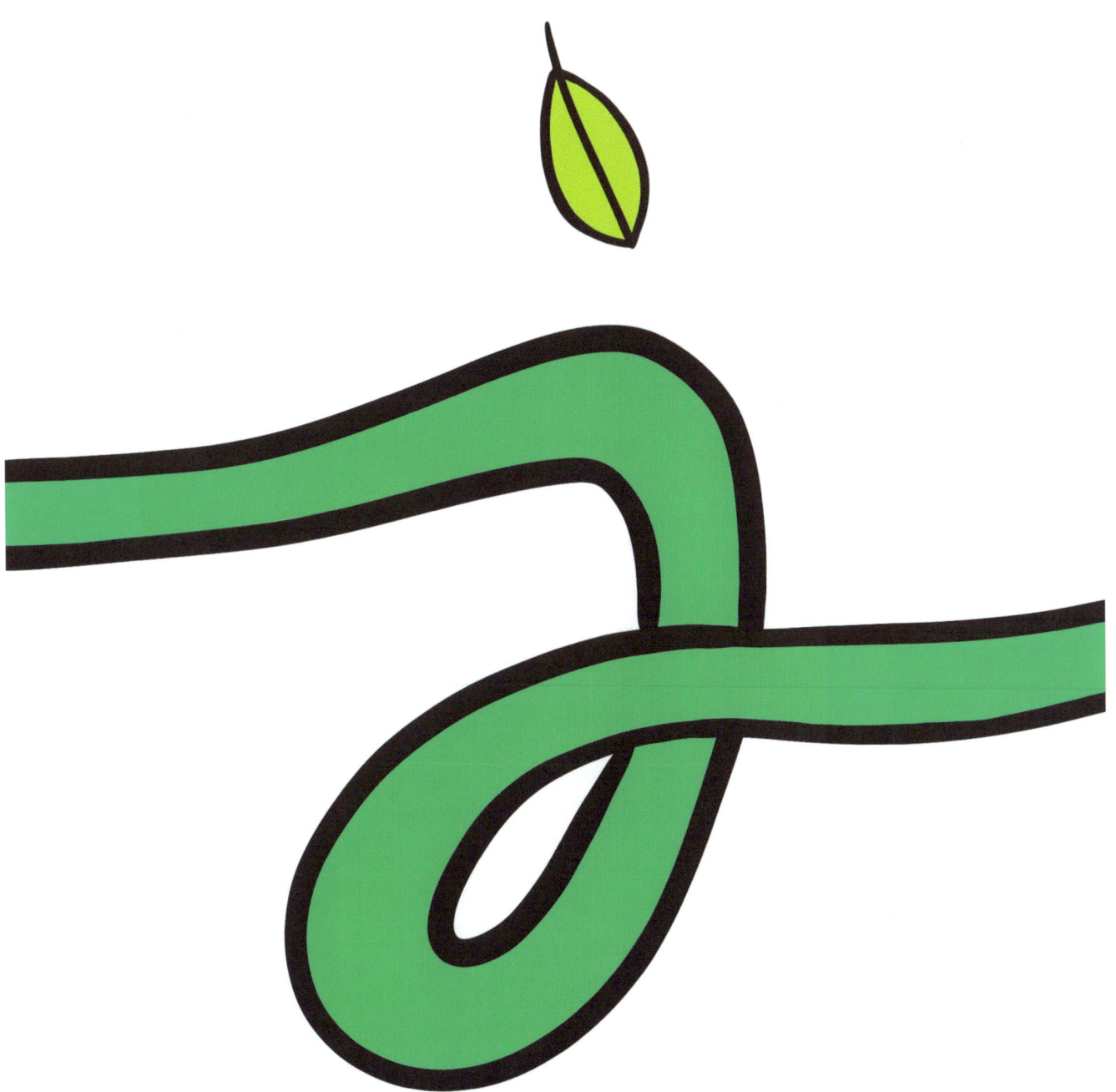

Young Picture Book Artists Program

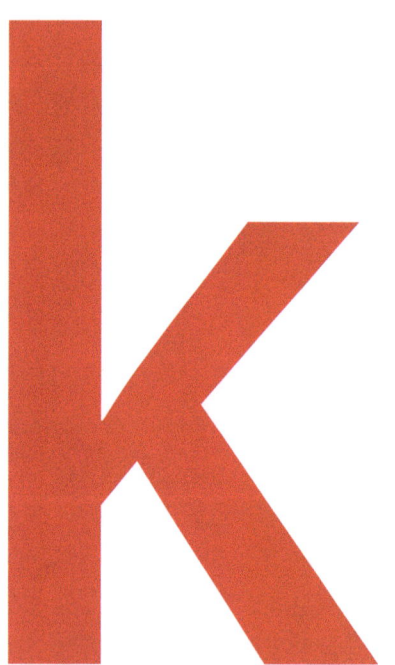

Young Picture Book Artists Program

The Cursive Lettered Snake

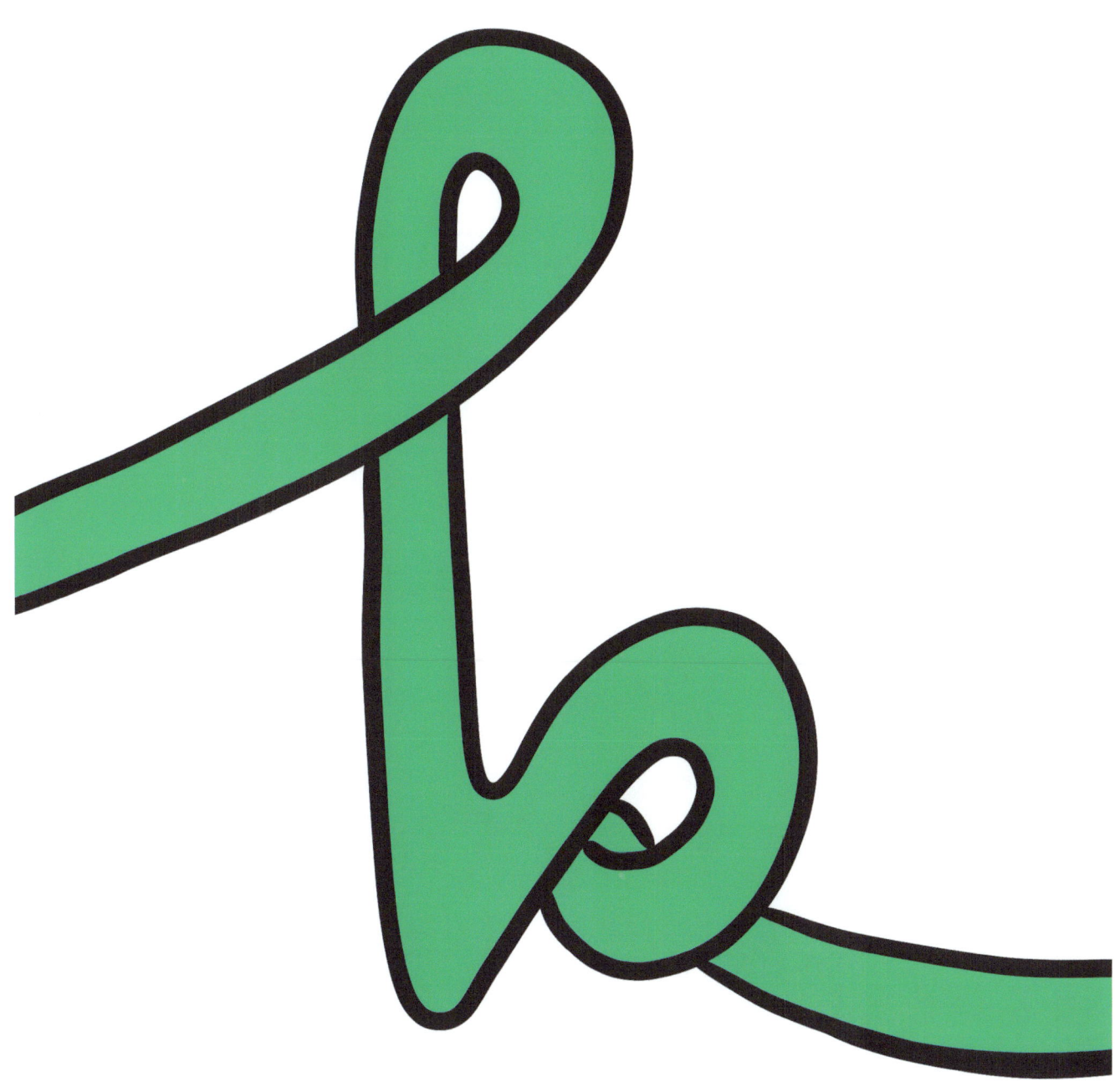

Young Picture Book Artists Program

Young Picture Book Artists Program

The Cursive Lettered Snake

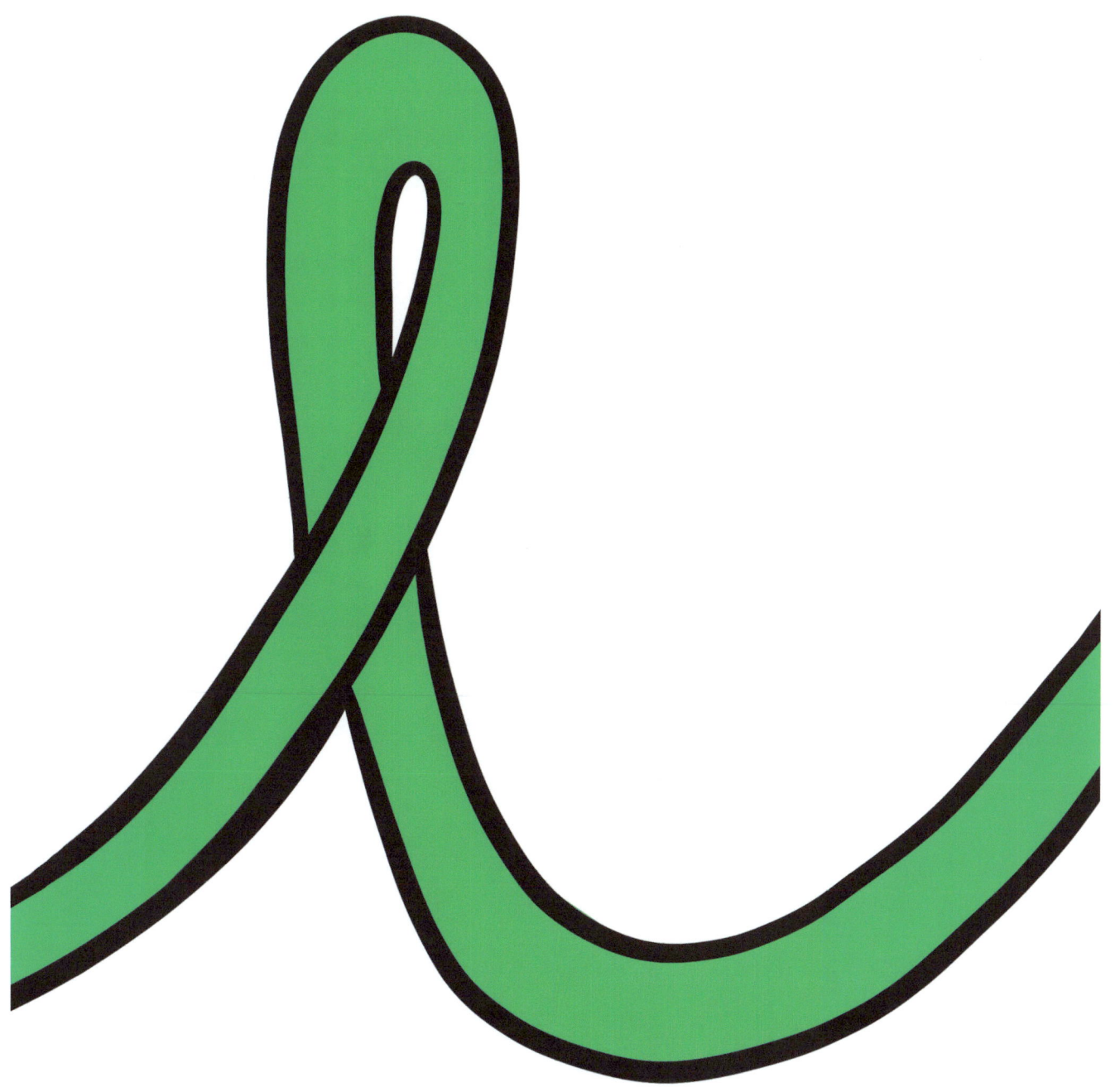

Young Picture Book Artists Program

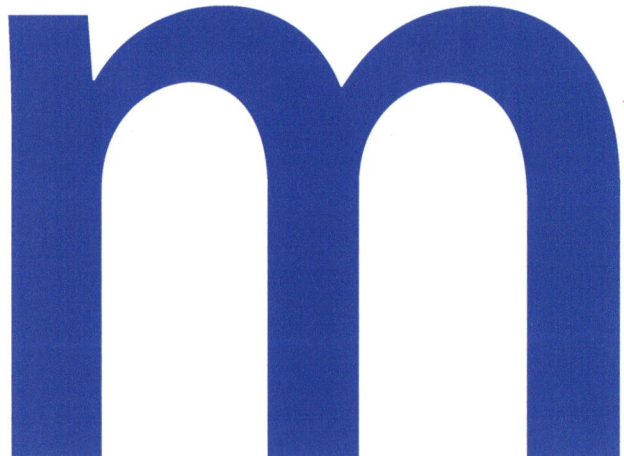

The Cursive Lettered Snake

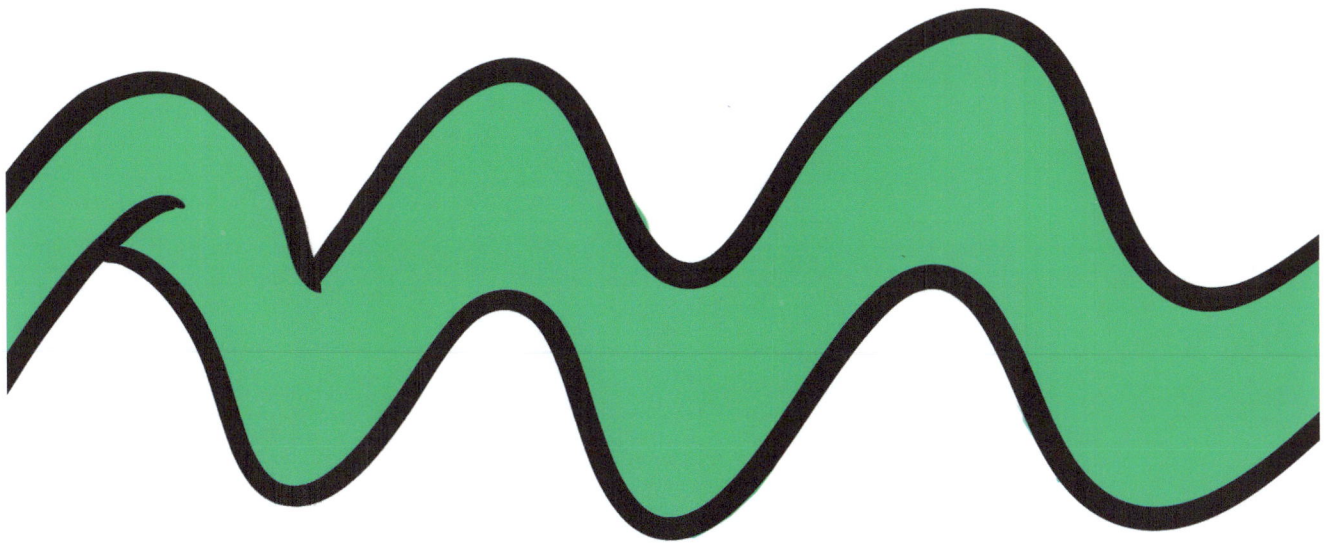

Young Picture Book Artists Program

The Cursive Lettered Snake

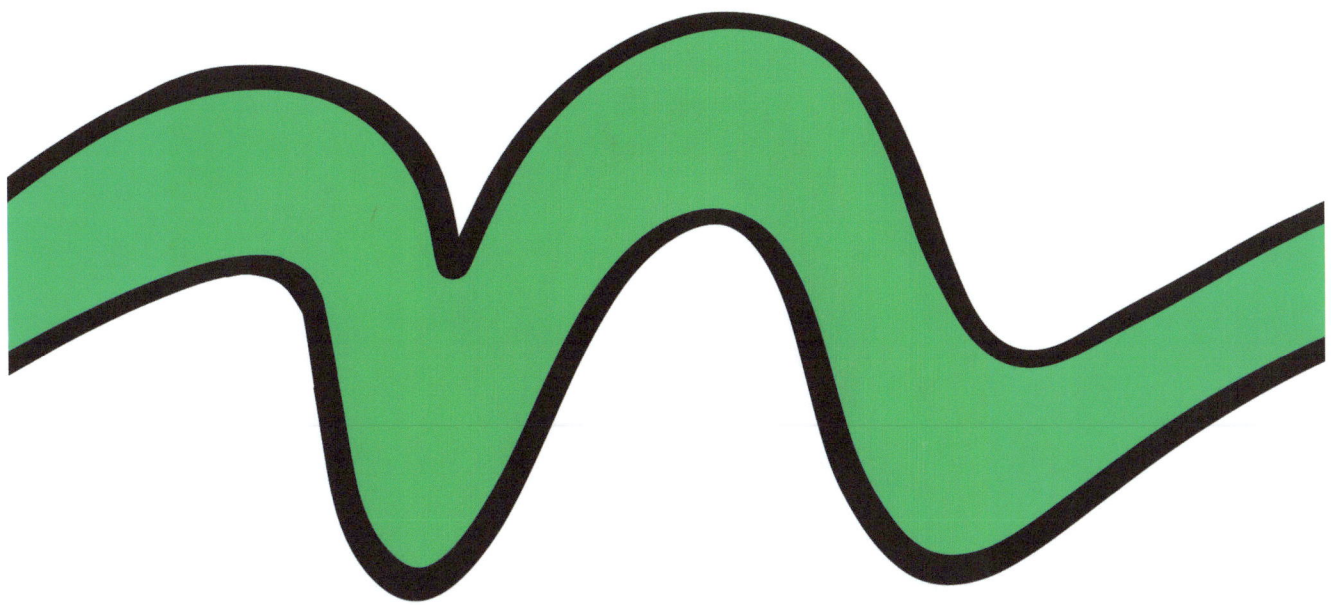

Young Picture Book Artists Program

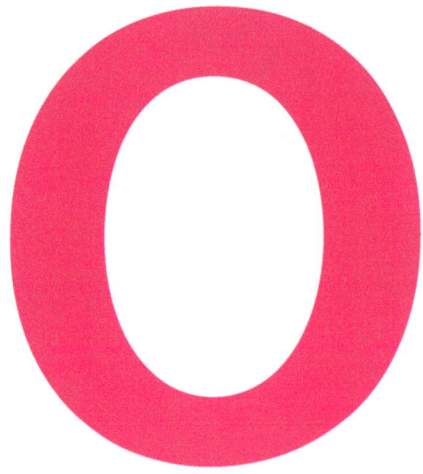

Young Picture Book Artists Program

The Cursive Lettered Snake

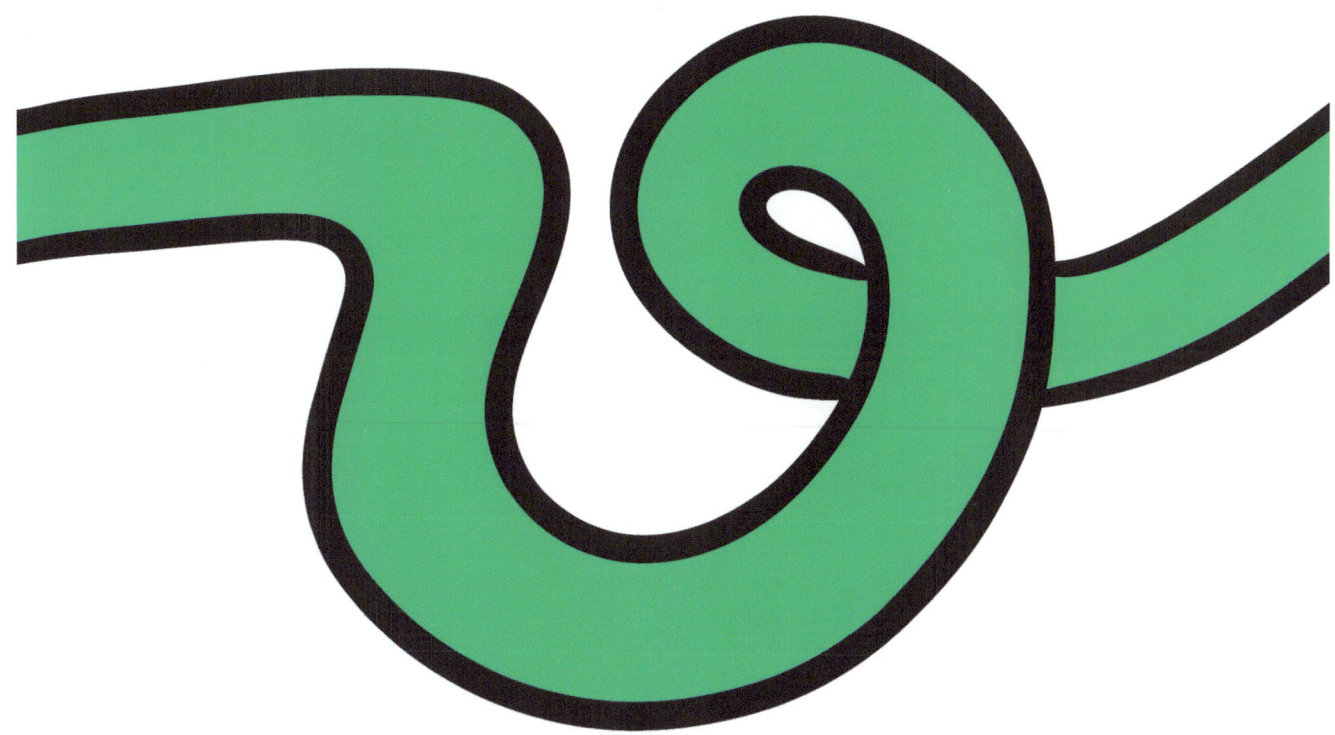

Young Picture Book Artists Program

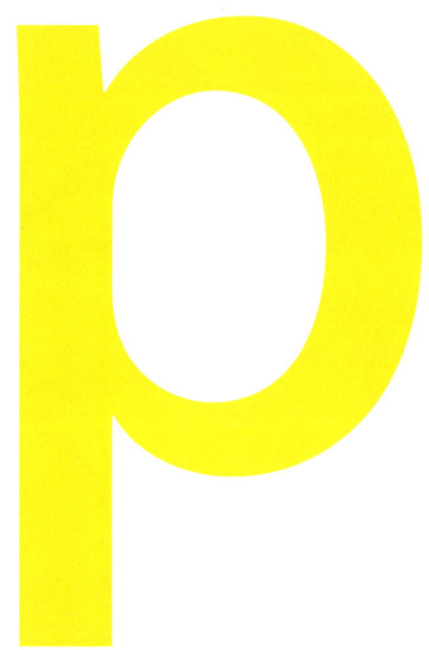

The Cursive Lettered Snake

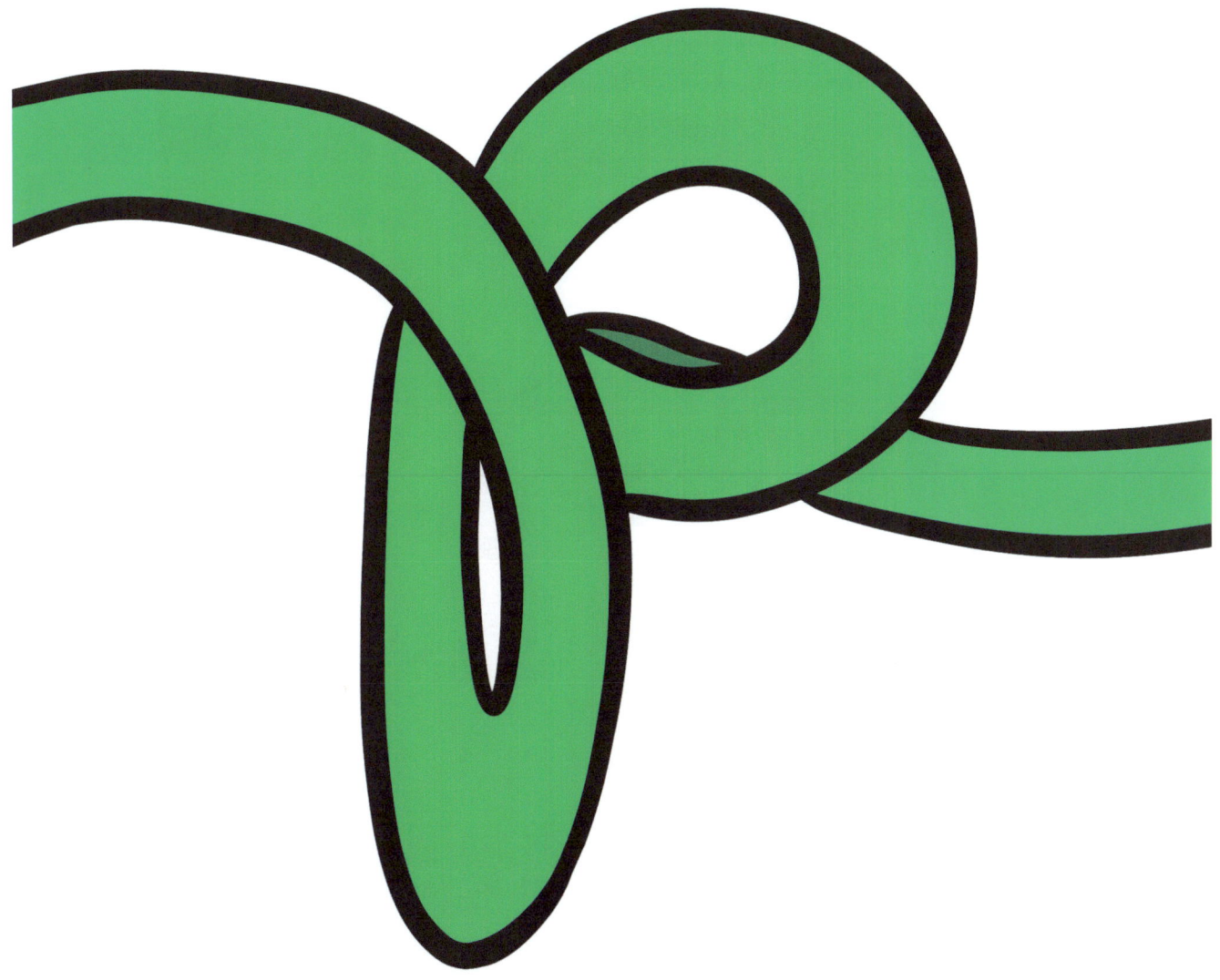

Young Picture Book Artists Program

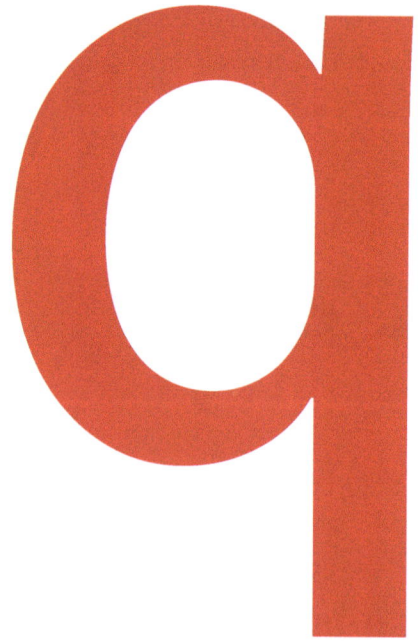

The Cursive Lettered Snake

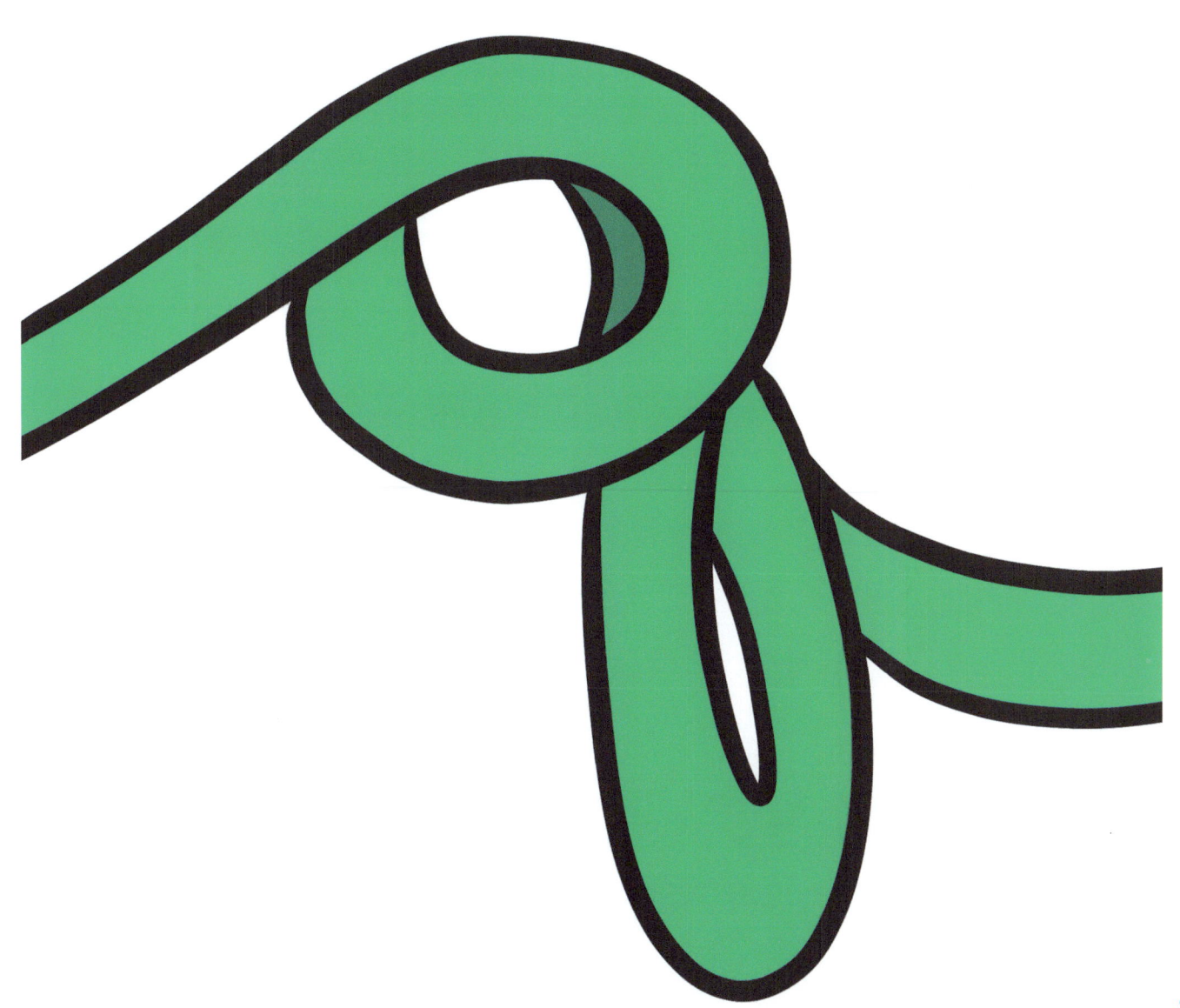

Young Picture Book Artists Program

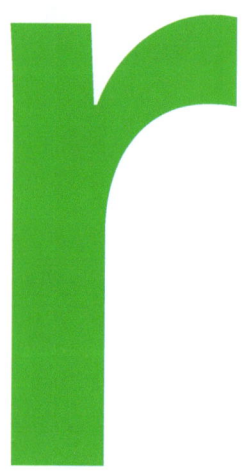

The Cursive Lettered Snake

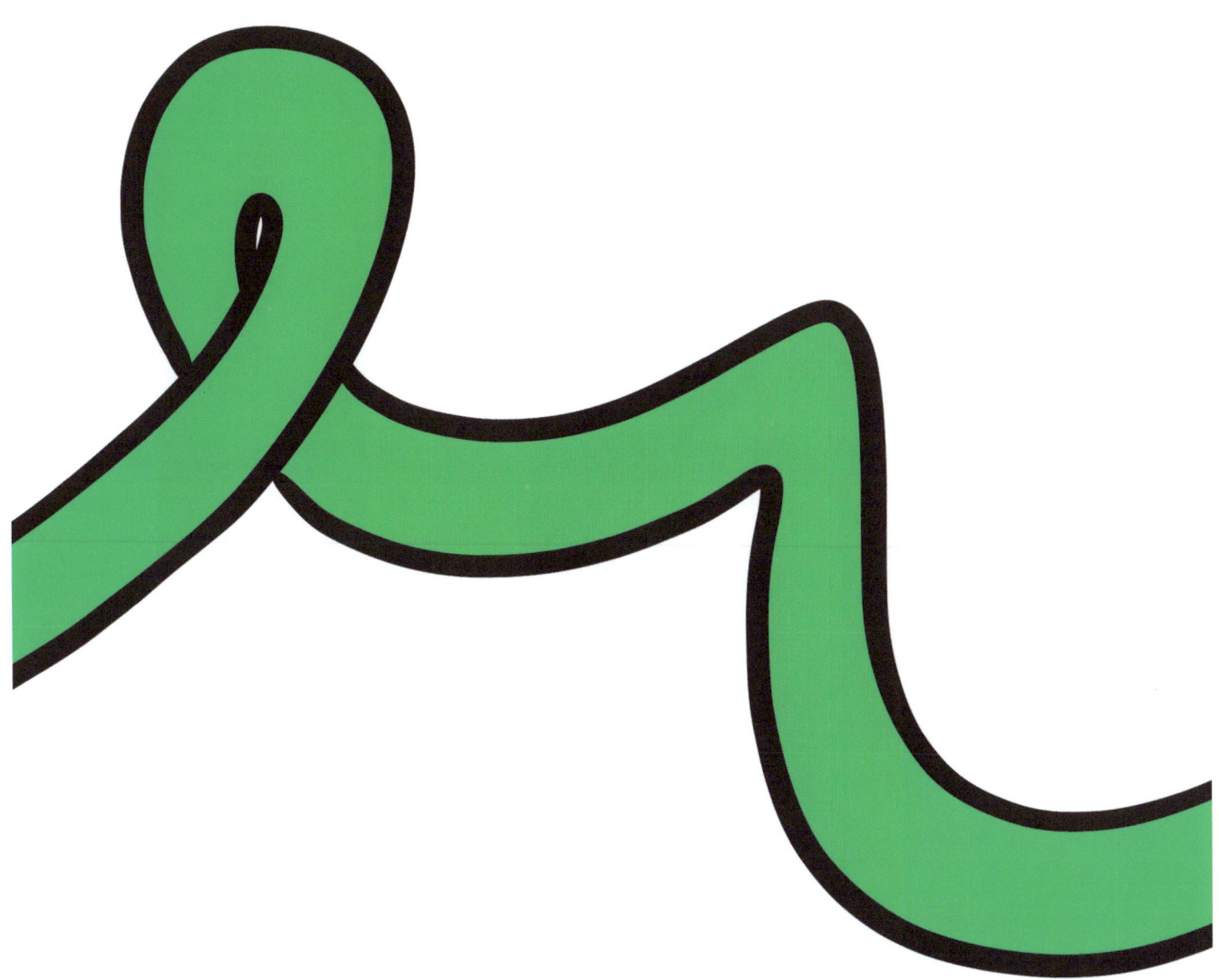

Young Picture Book Artists Program

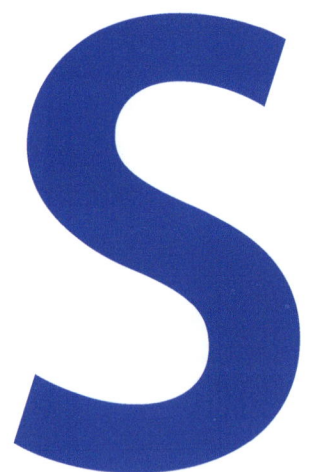

The Cursive Lettered Snake

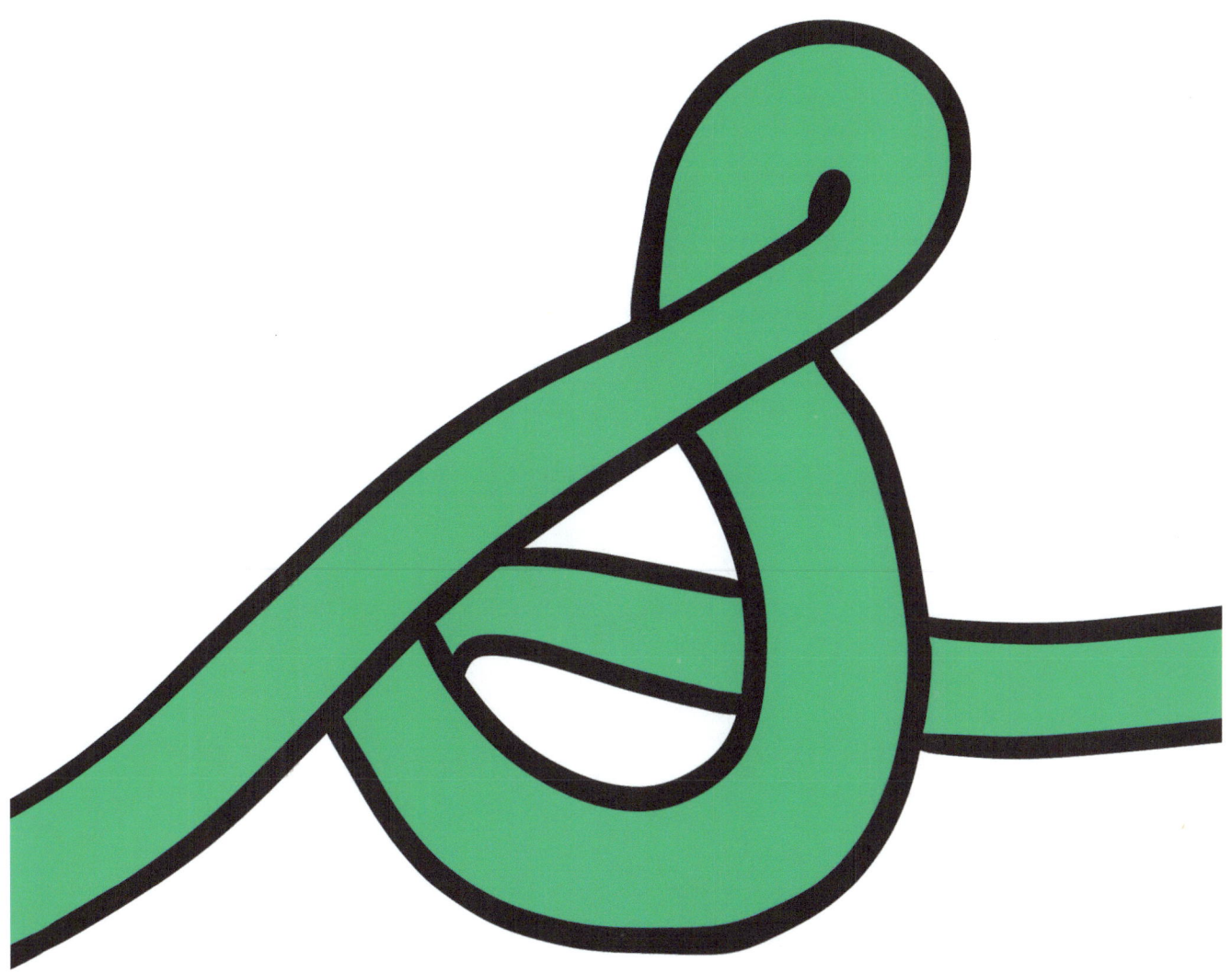

Young Picture Book Artists Program

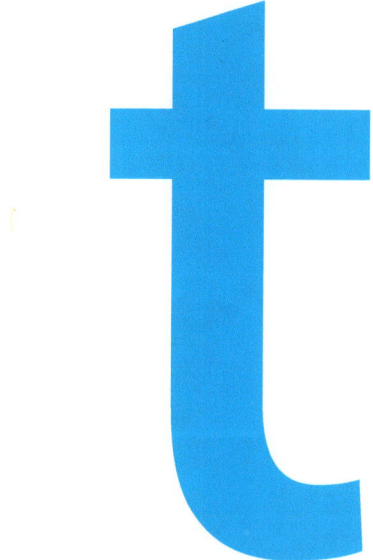

The Cursive Lettered Snake

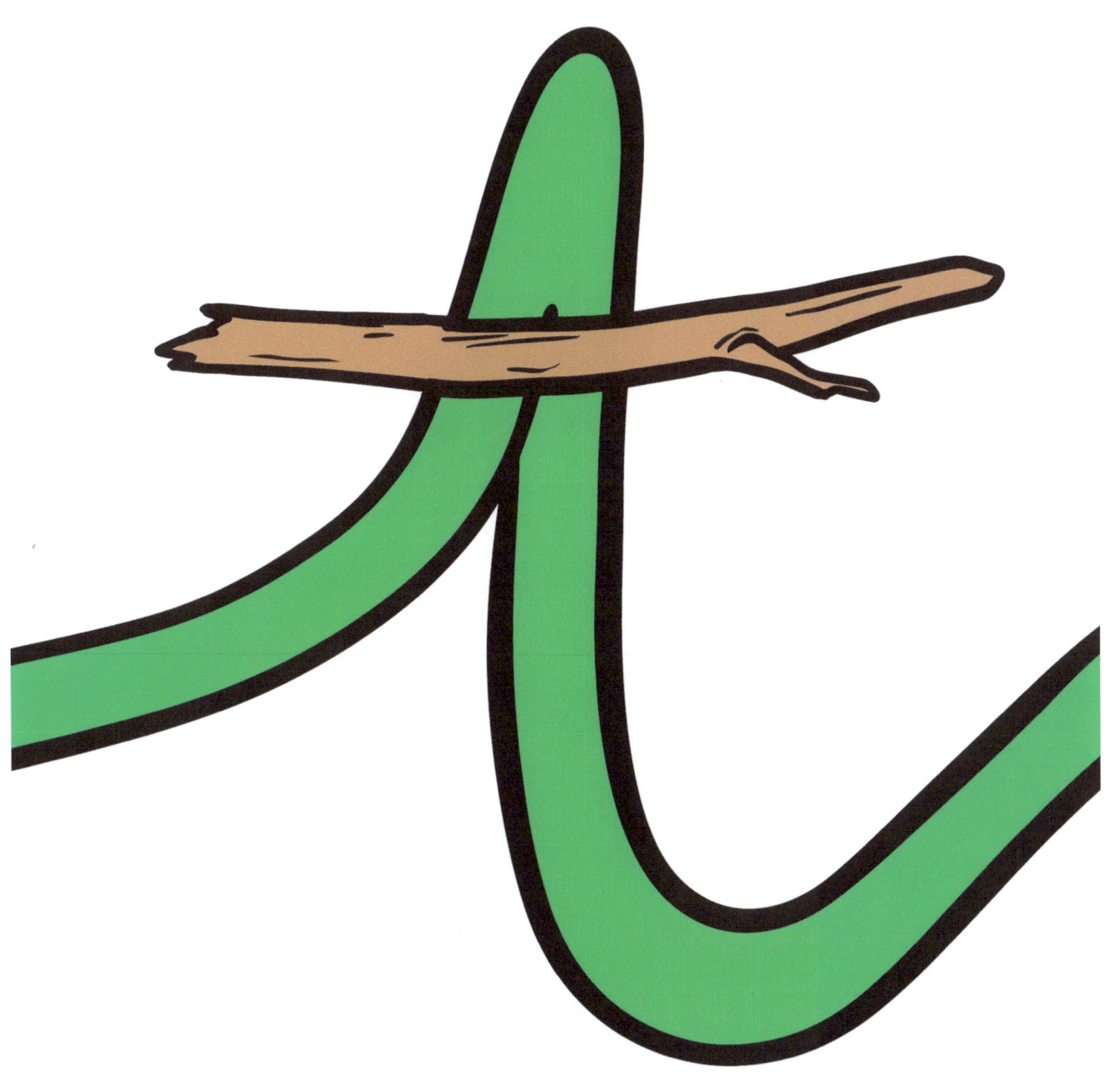

Young Picture Book Artists Program

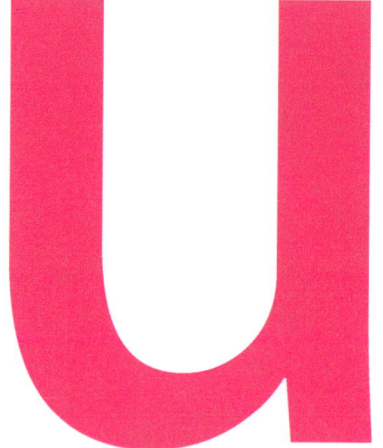

The Cursive Lettered Snake

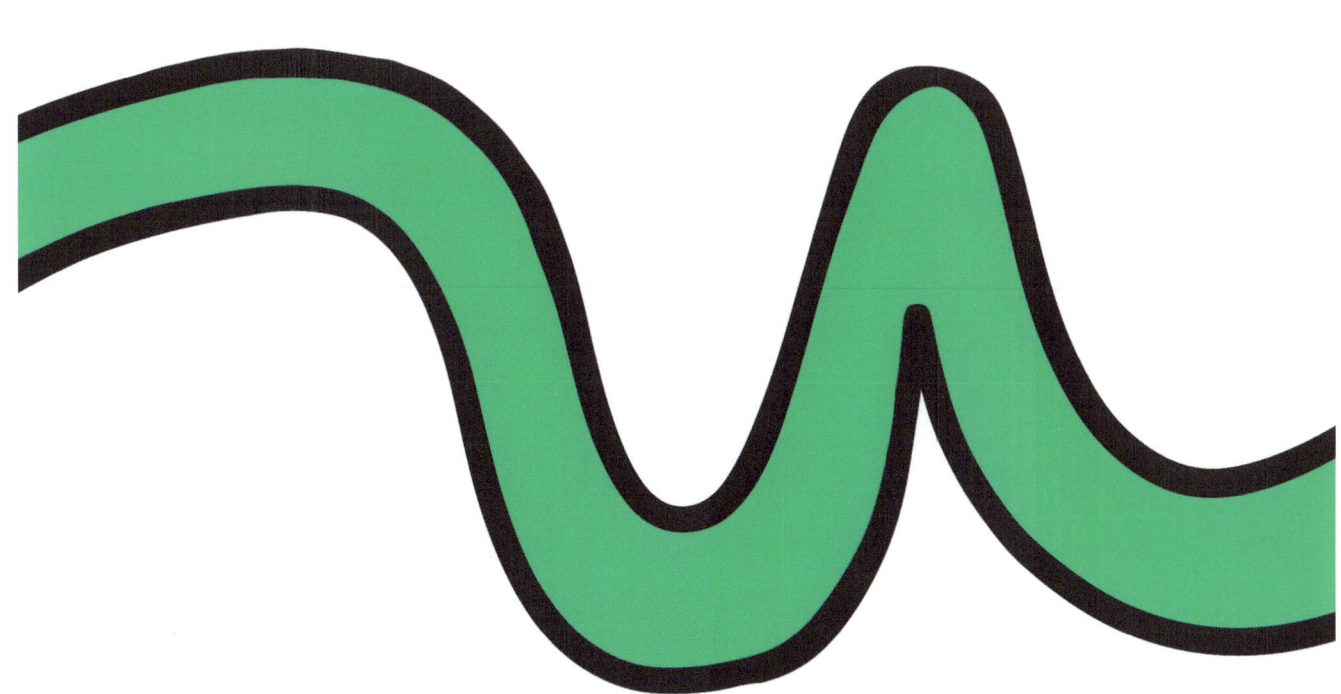

Young Picture Book Artists Program

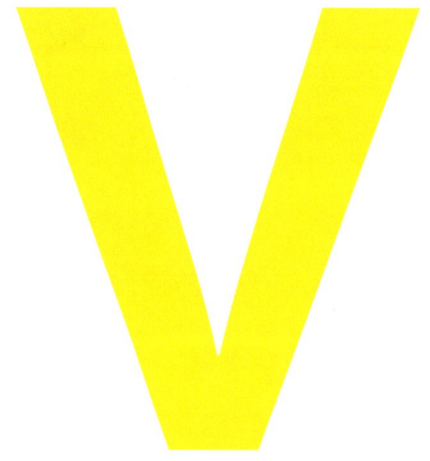

Young Picture Book Artists Program

The Cursive Lettered Snake

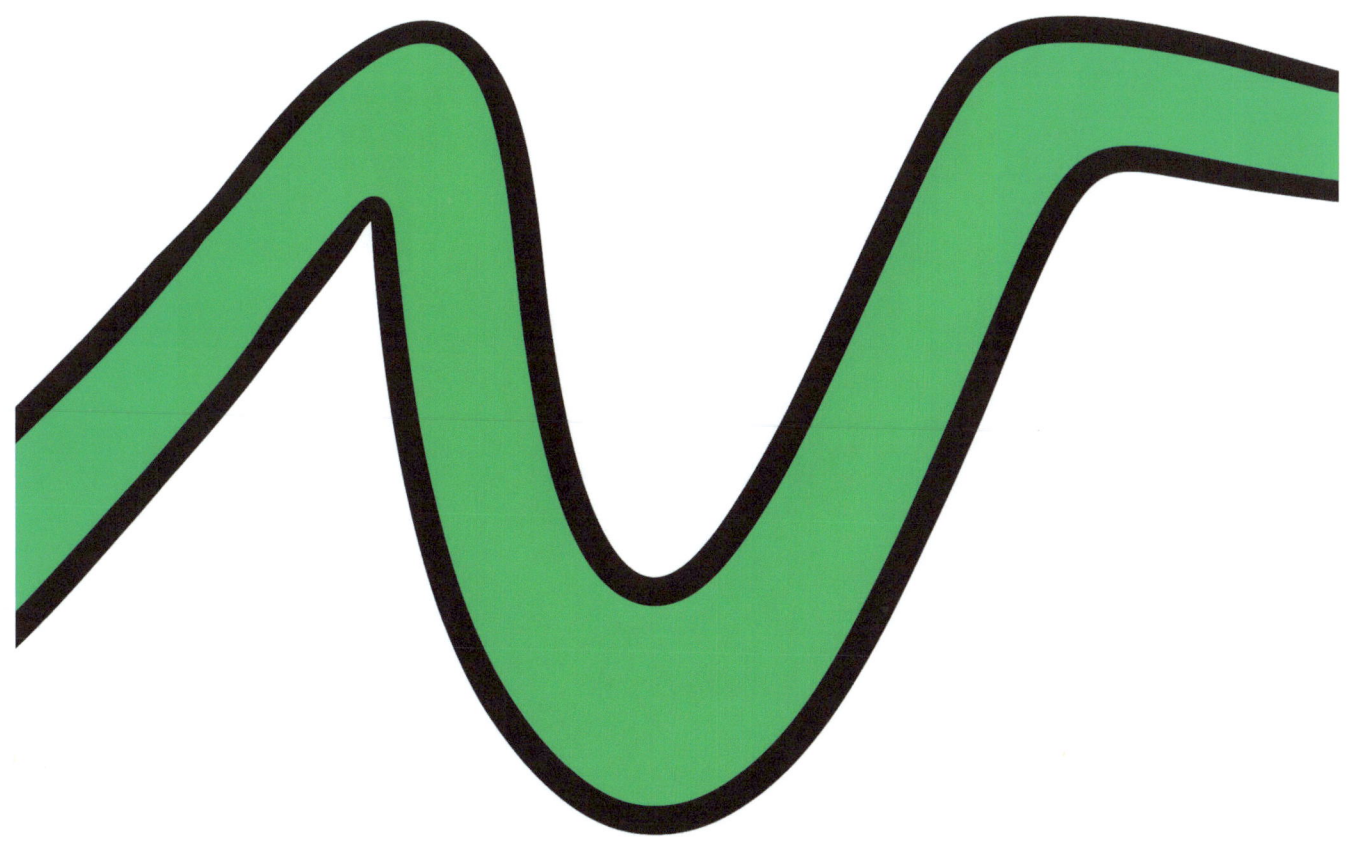

Young Picture Book Artists Program

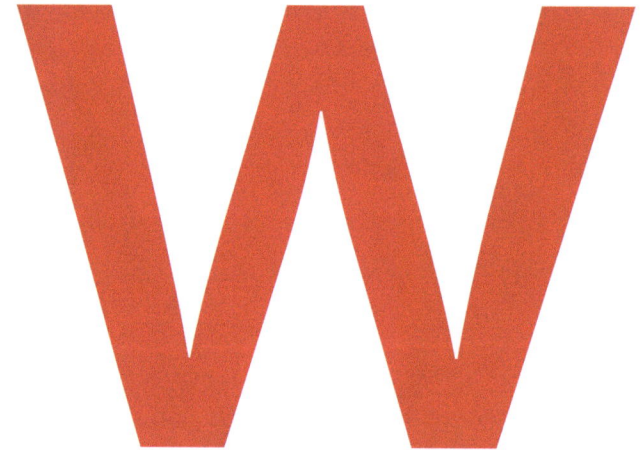

The Cursive Lettered Snake

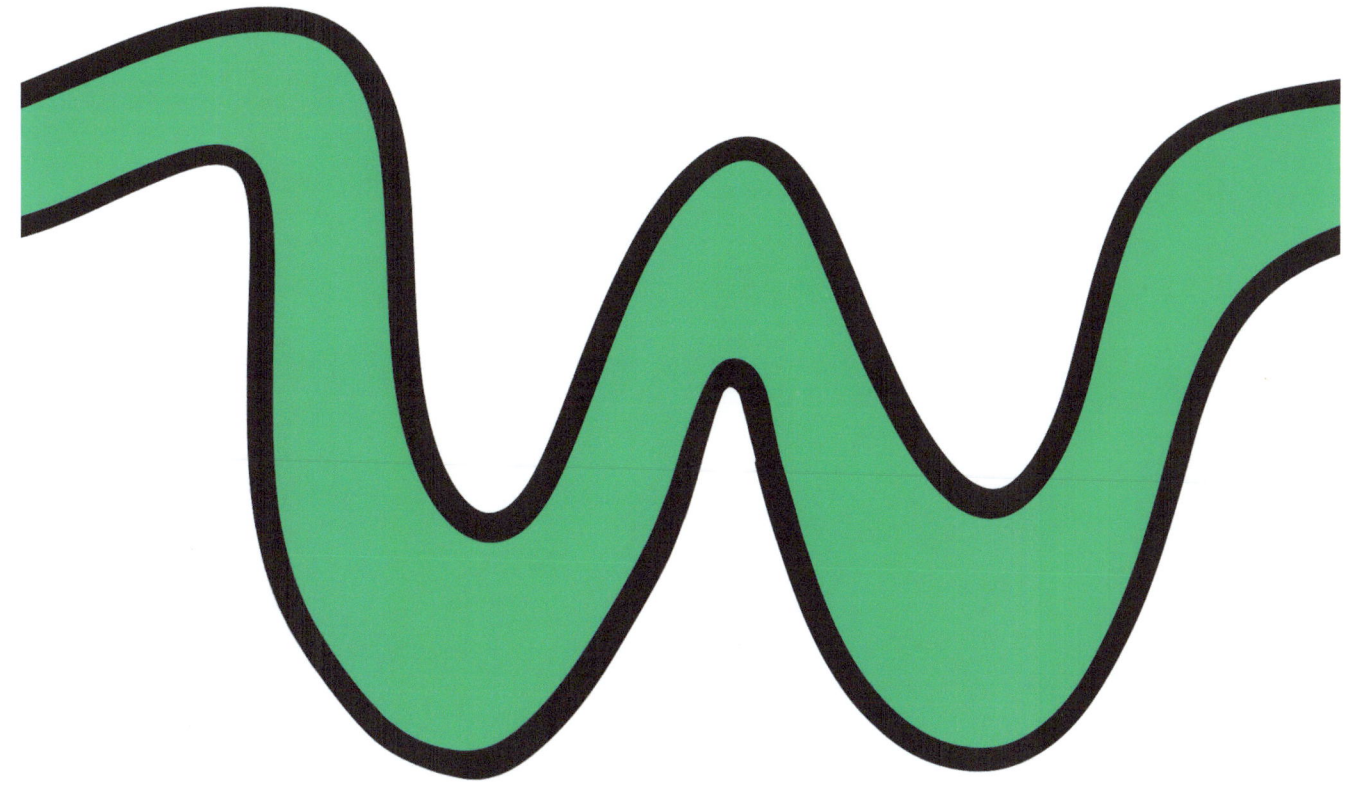

Young Picture Book Artists Program

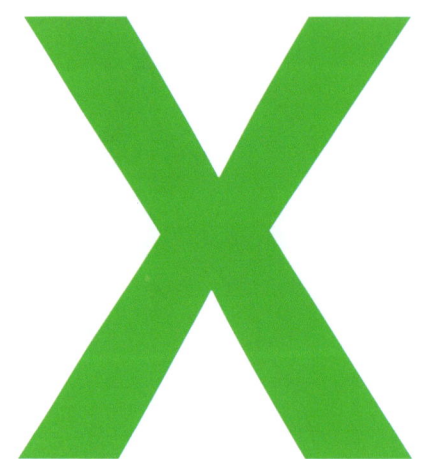

Young Picture Book Artists Program

The Cursive Lettered Snake

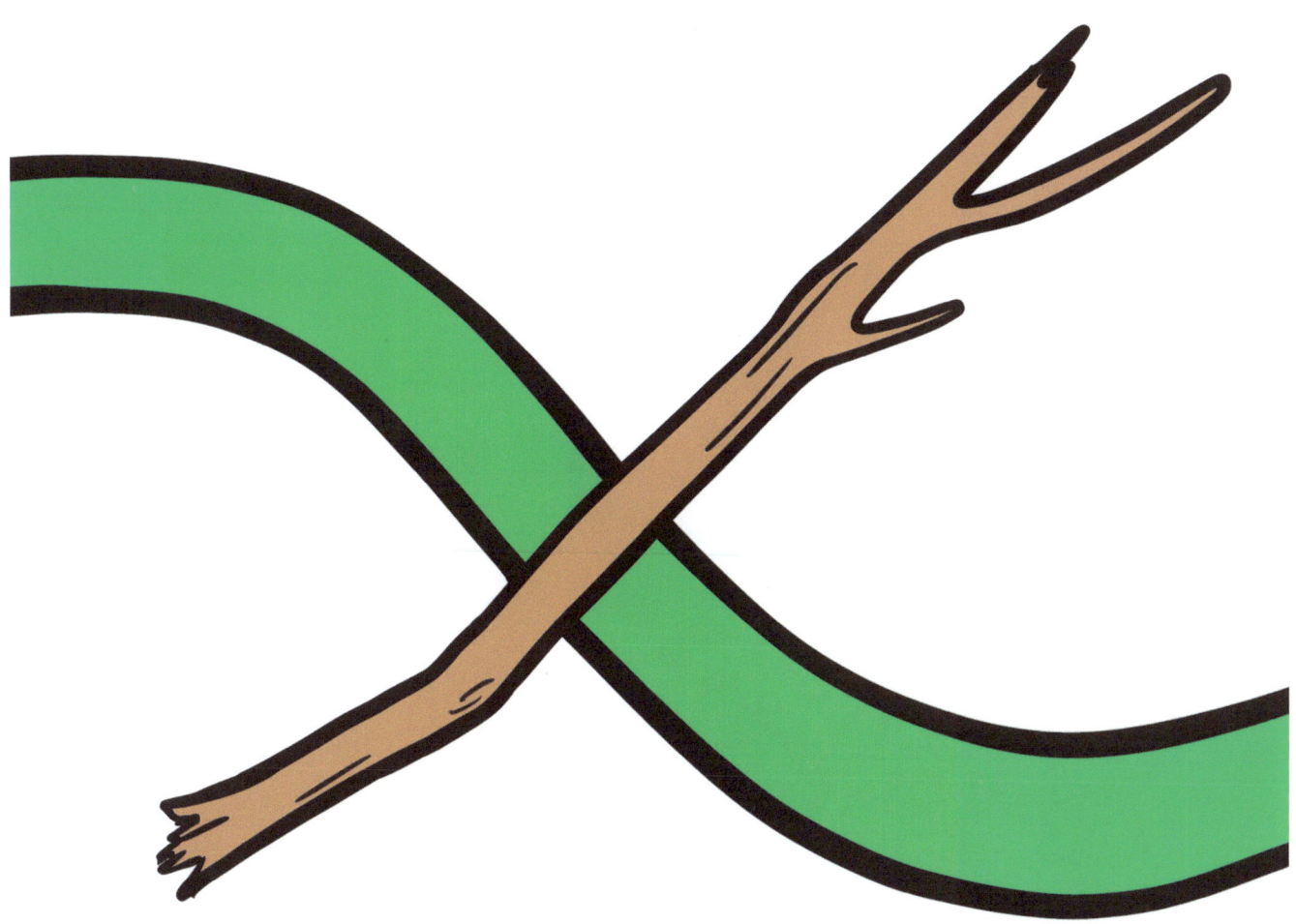

Young Picture Book Artists Program

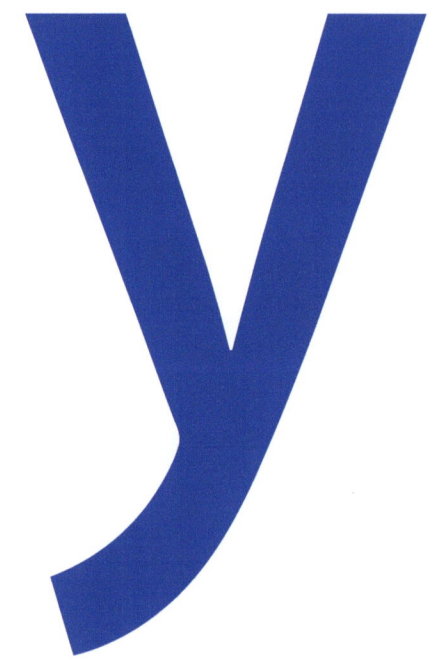

The Cursive Lettered Snake

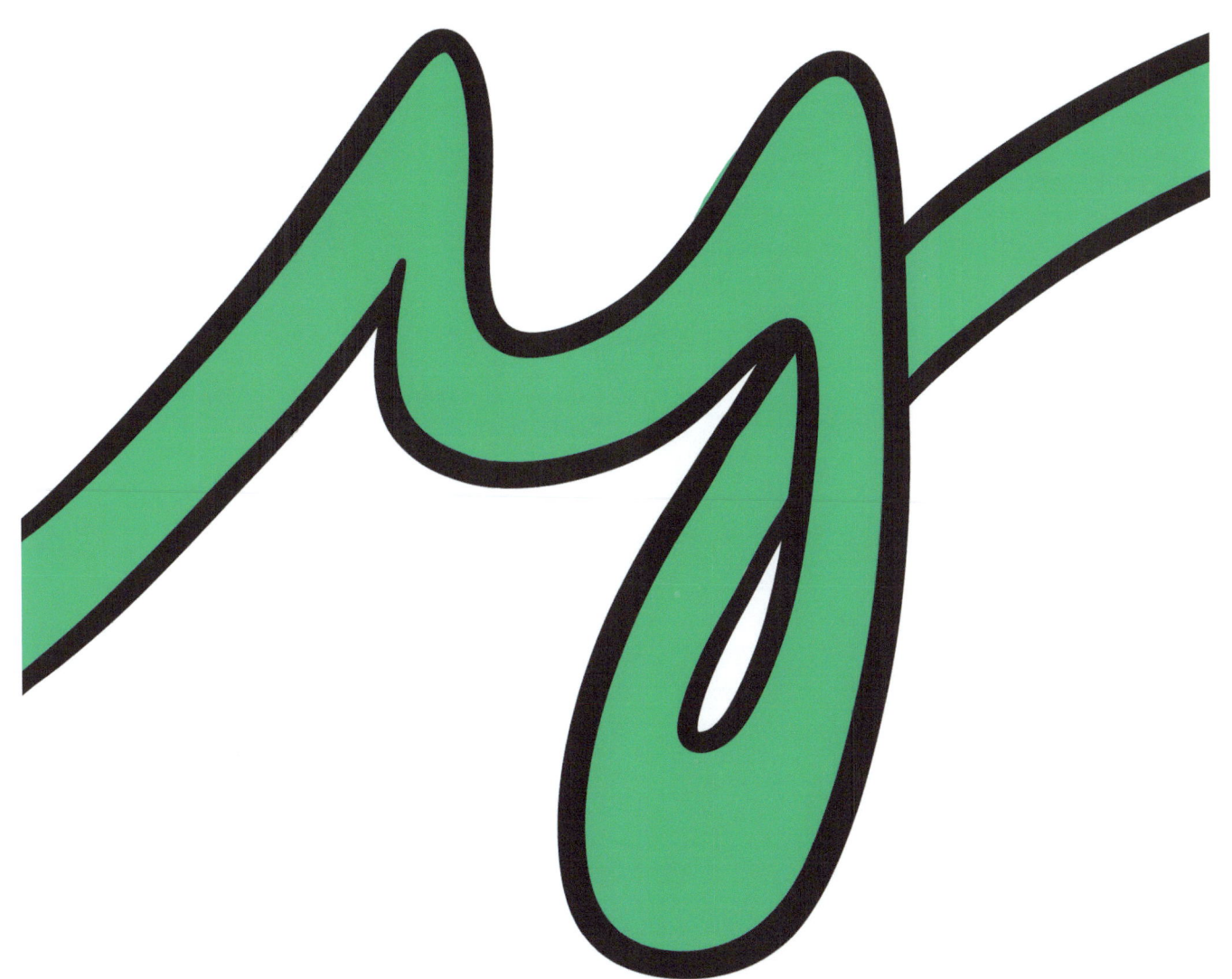

Young Picture Book Artists Program

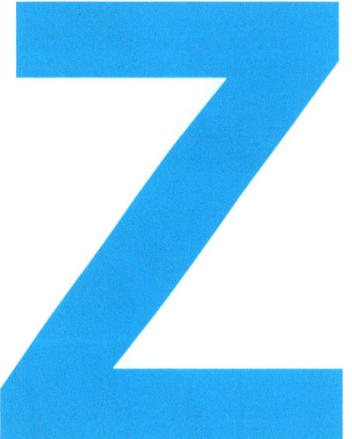

The Cursive Lettered Snake

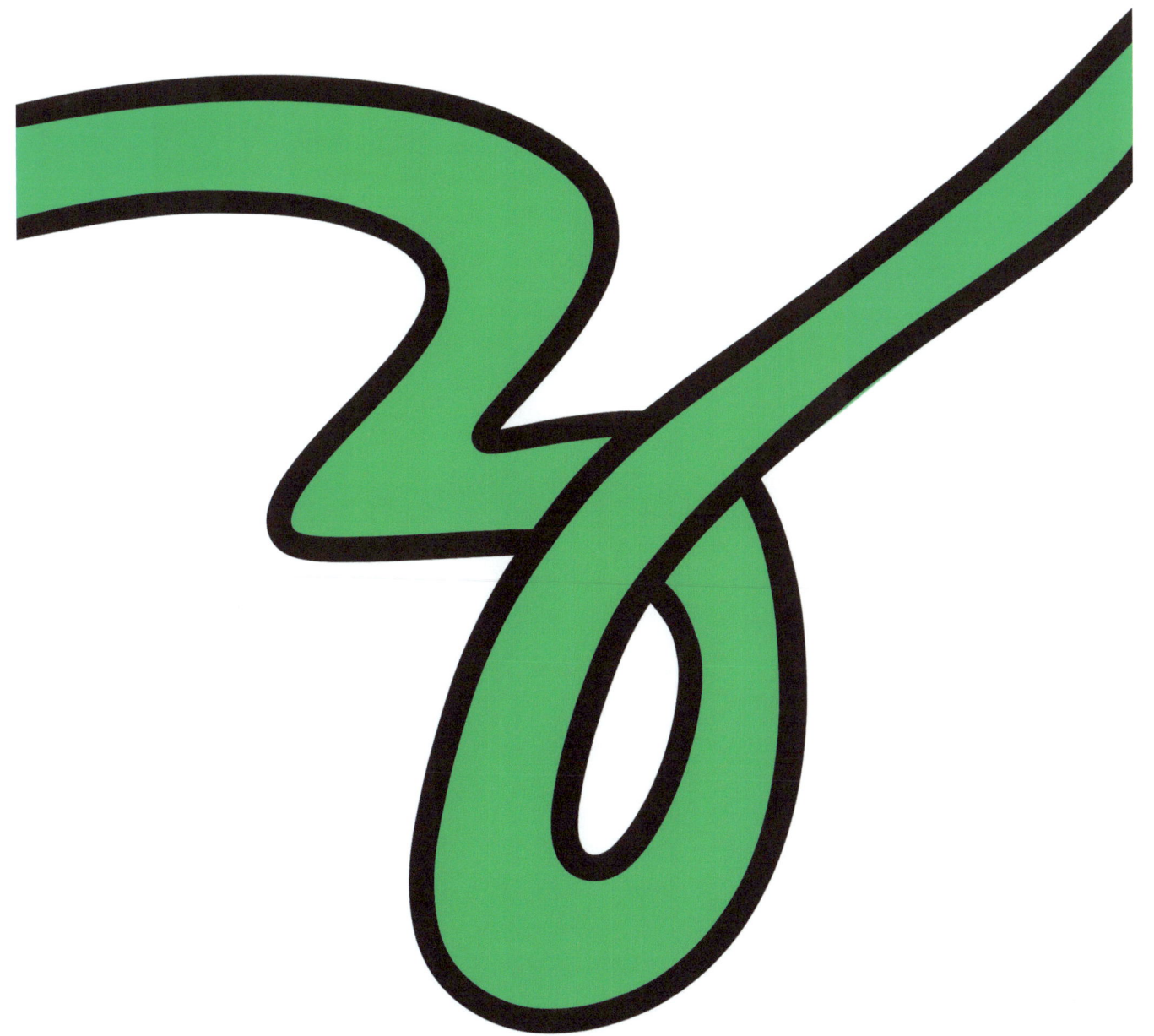

Young Picture Book Artists Program

The Cursive Lettered Snake

THE CURSIVE LETTERED SNAKE

Young Picture Book Artists Program

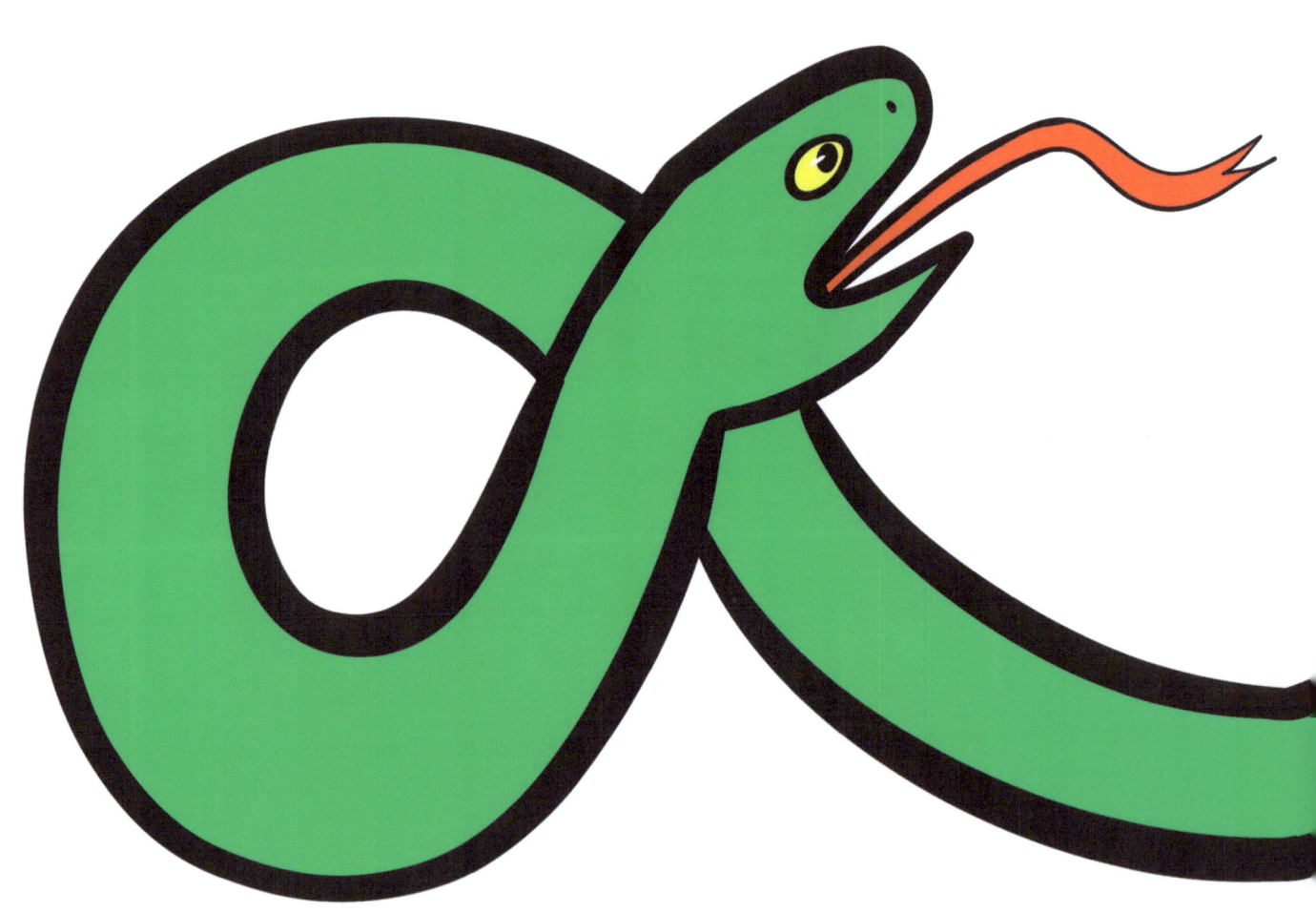

The Cursive Lettered Snake

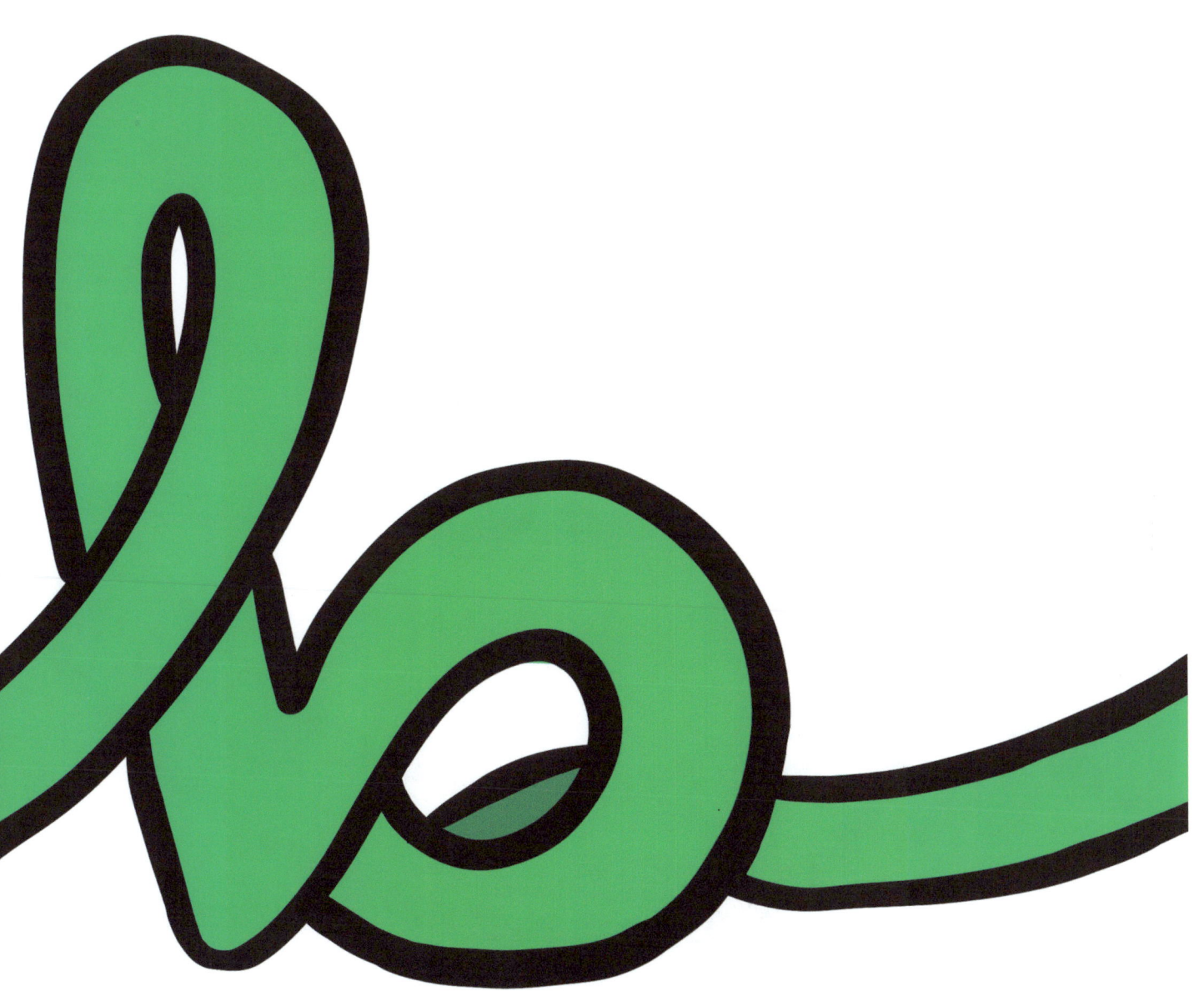

Young Picture Book Artists Program

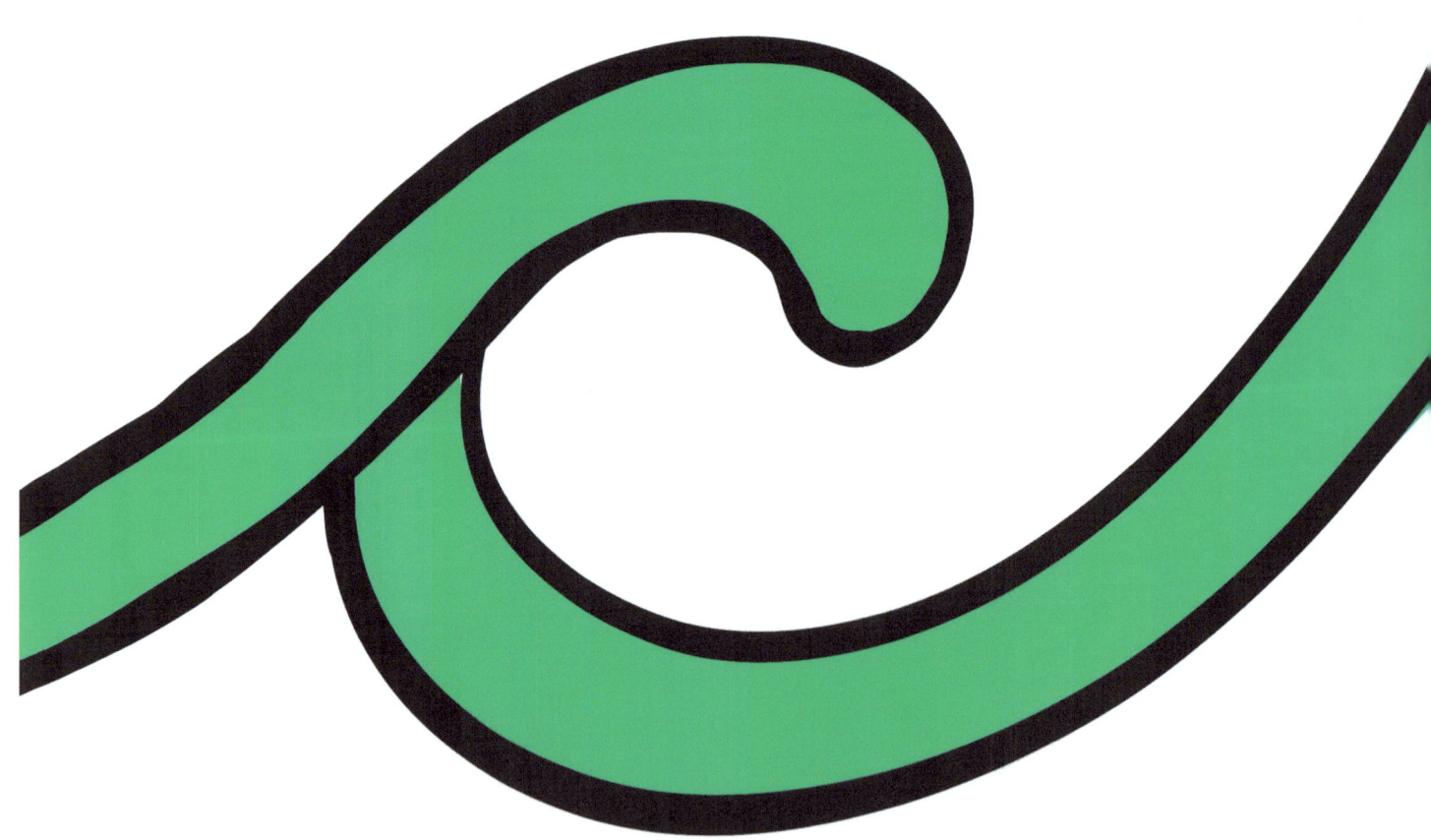

The Cursive Lettered Snake

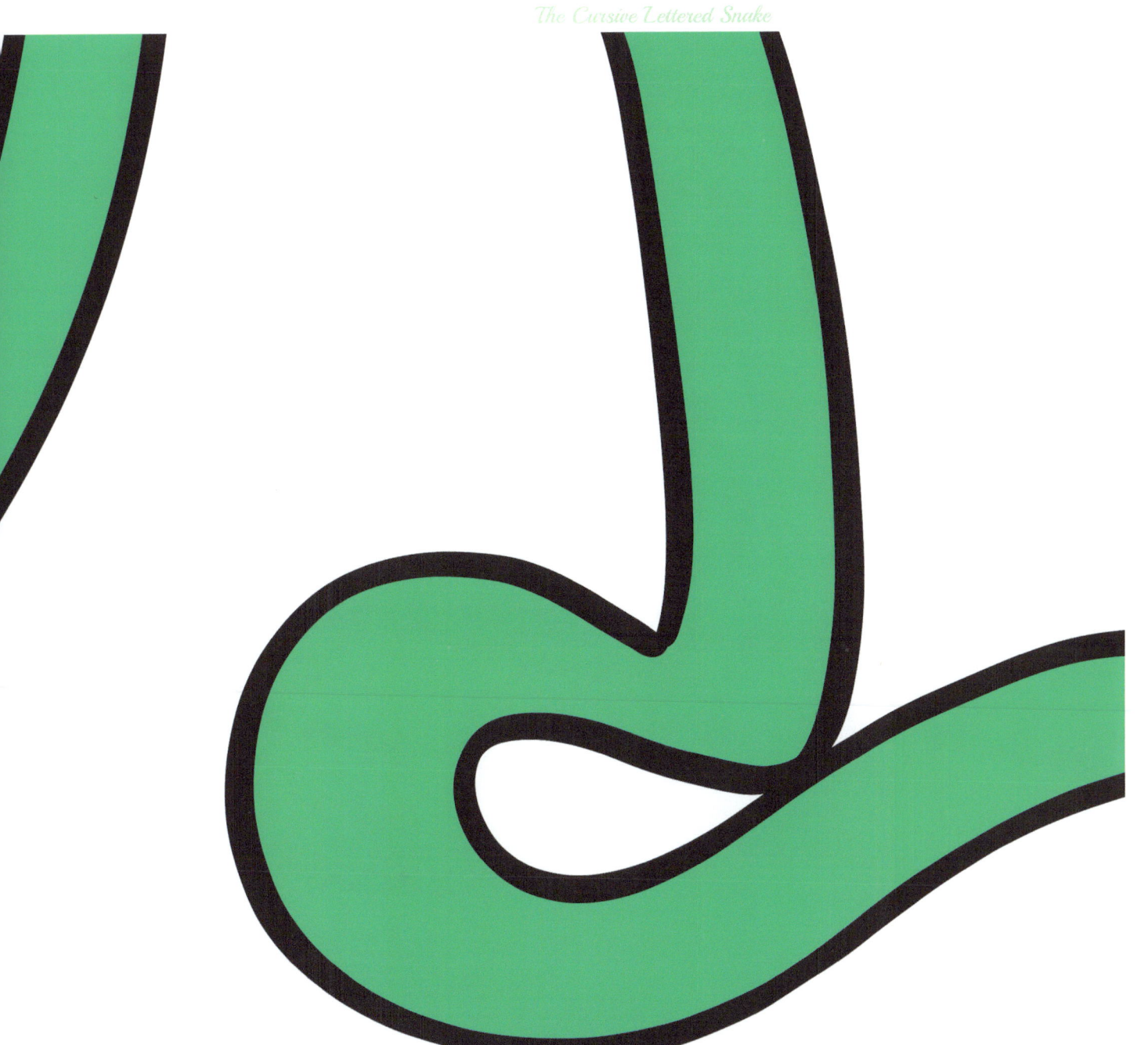

Young Picture Book Artists Program

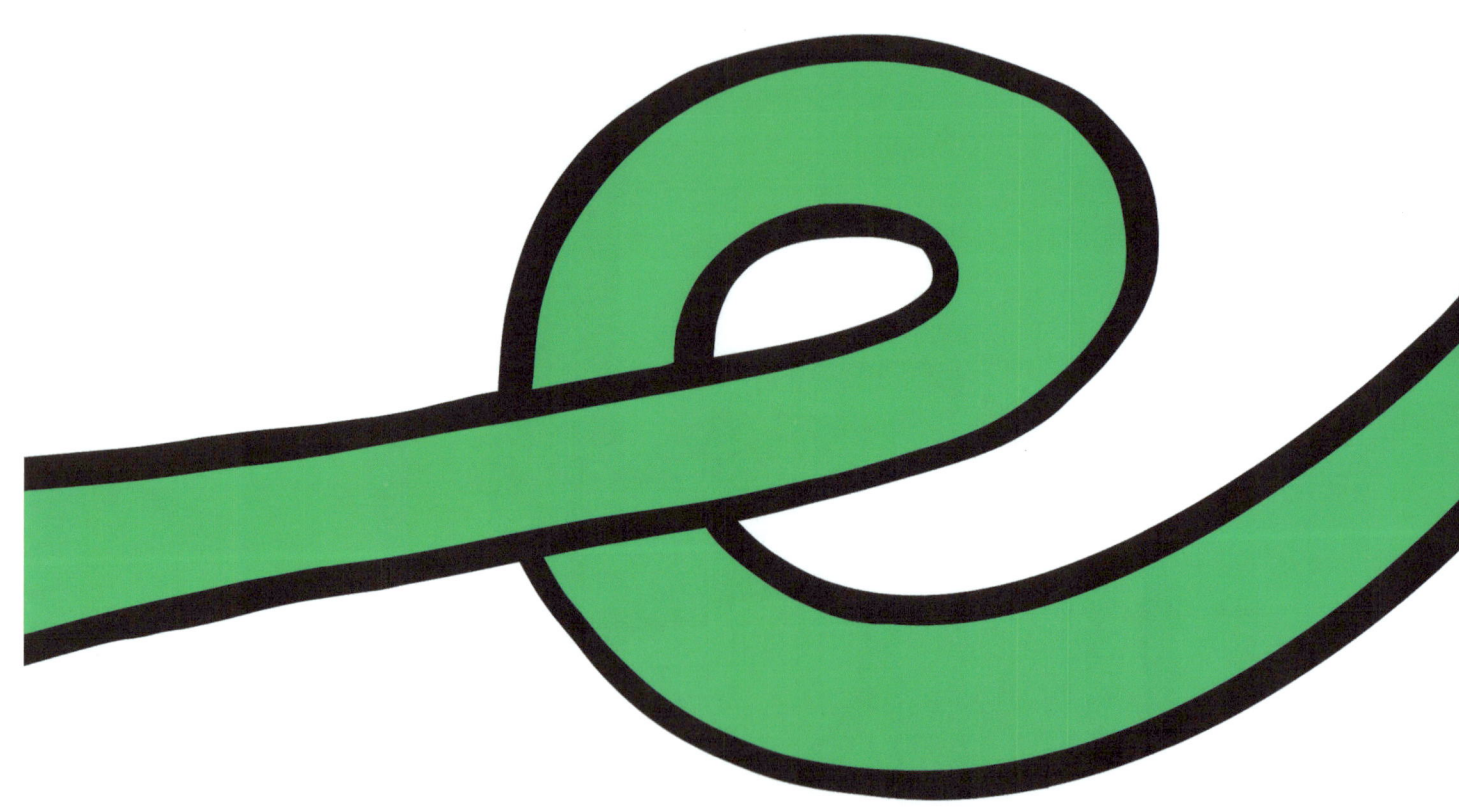

The Cursive Lettered Snake

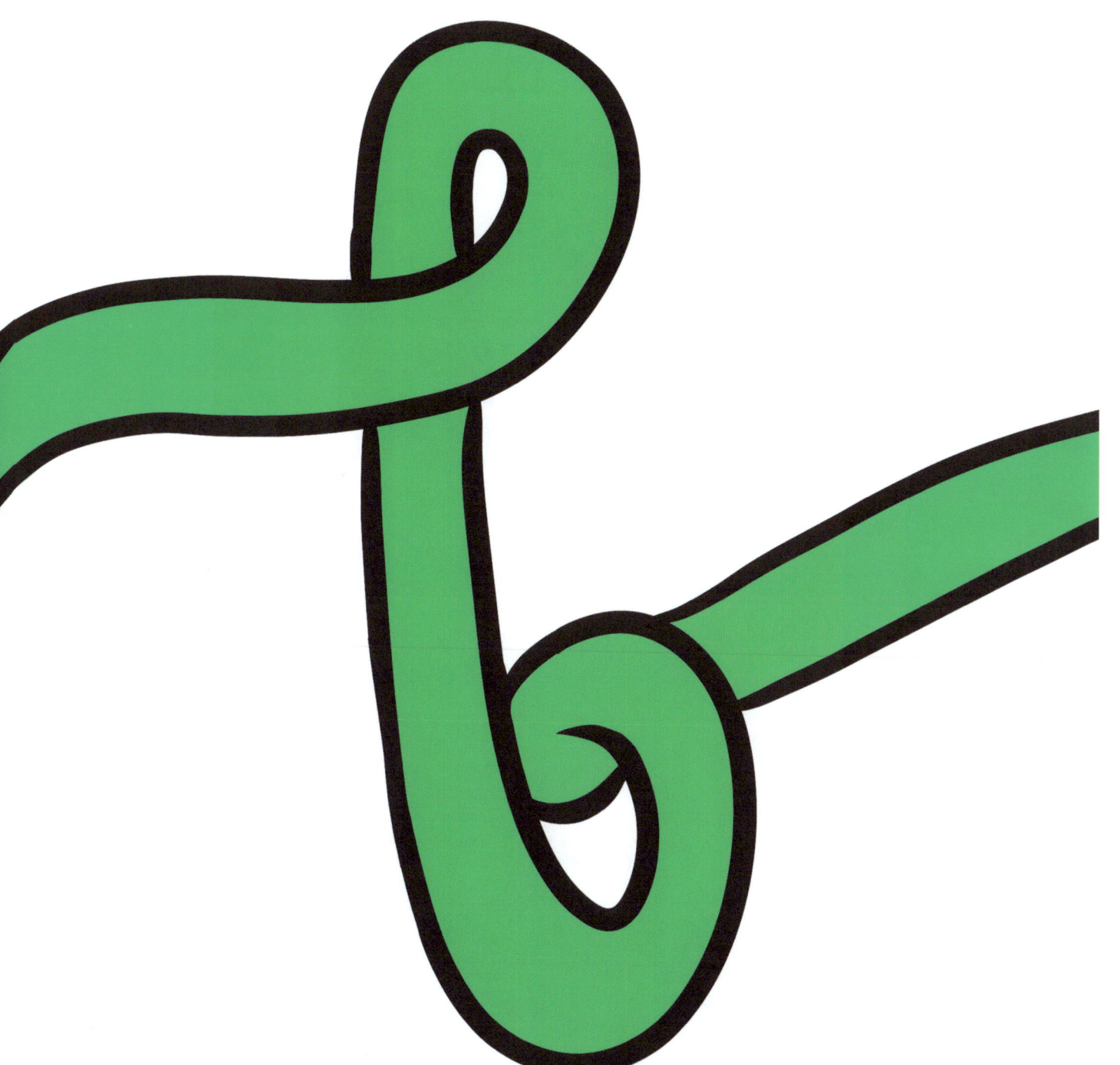

Young Picture Book Artists Program

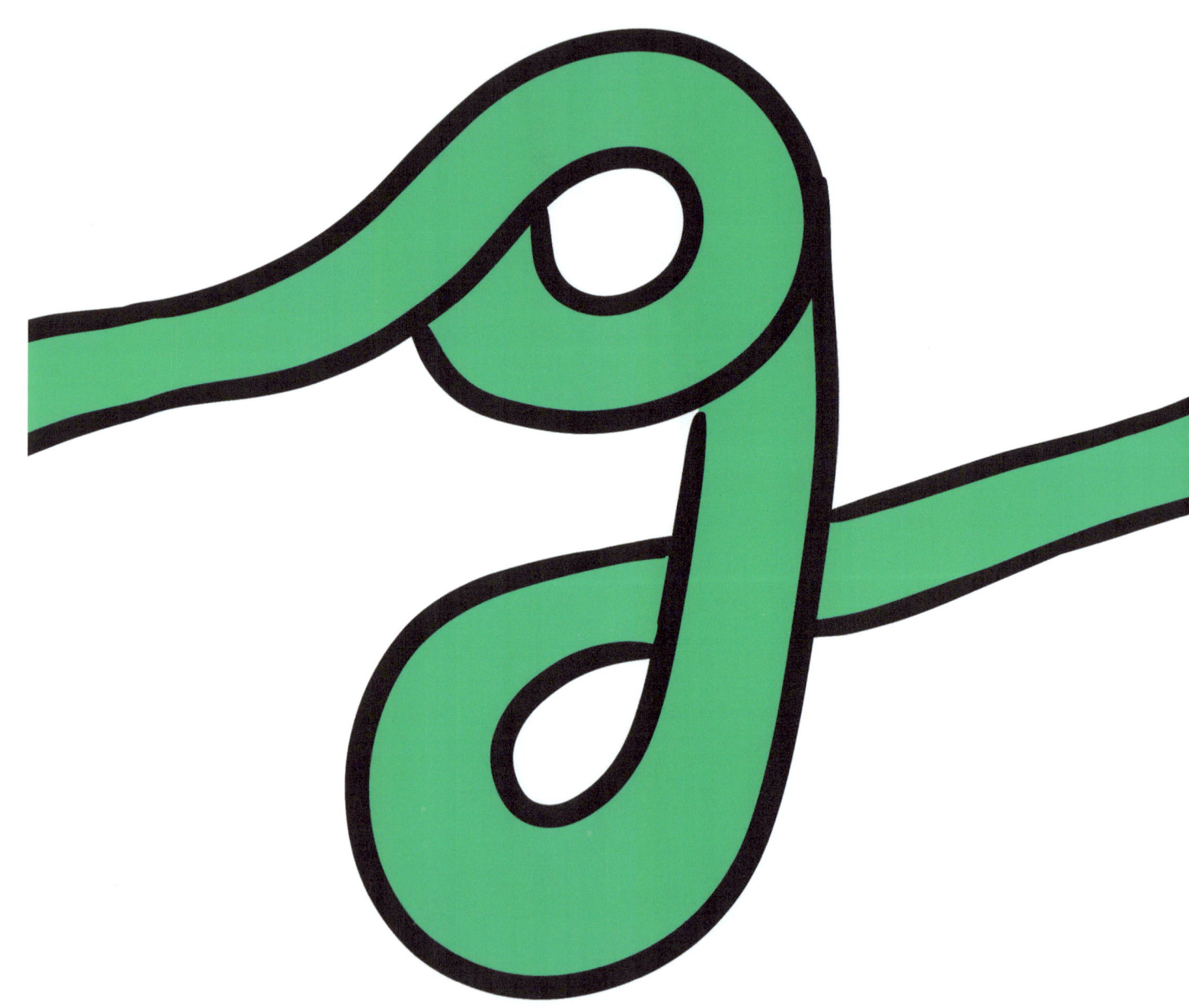

The Cursive Lettered Snake

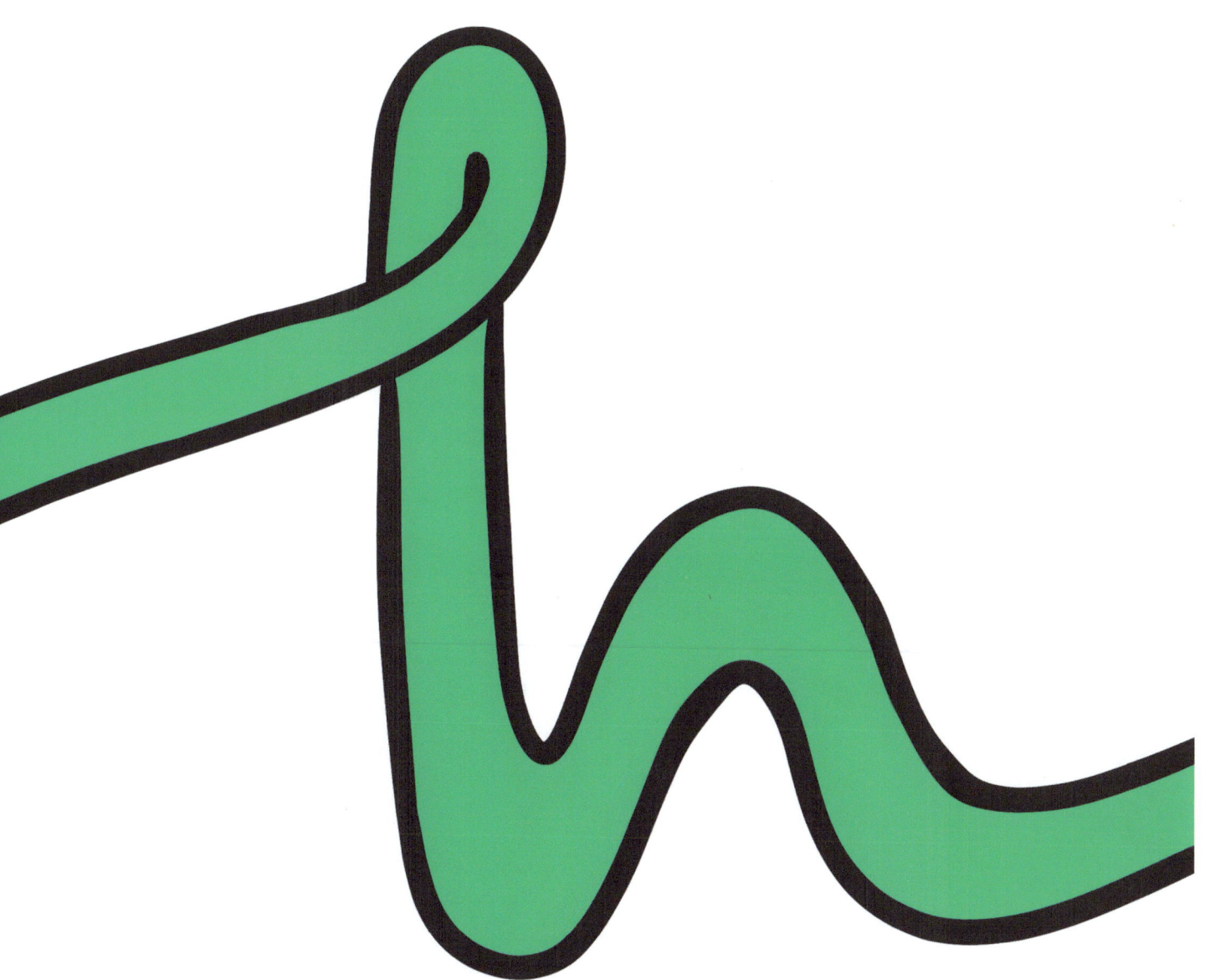

Young Picture Book Artists Program

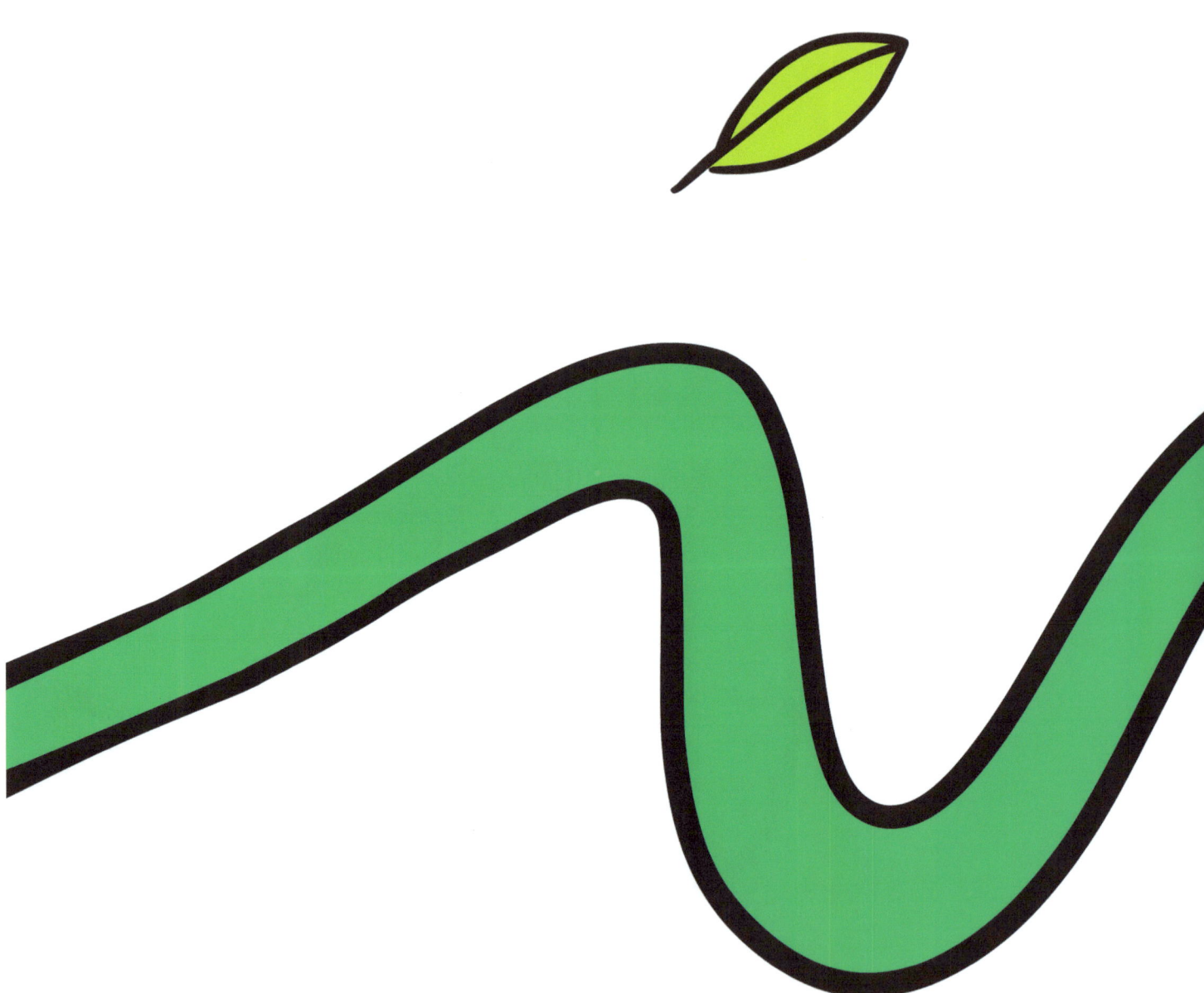

The Cursive Lettered Snake

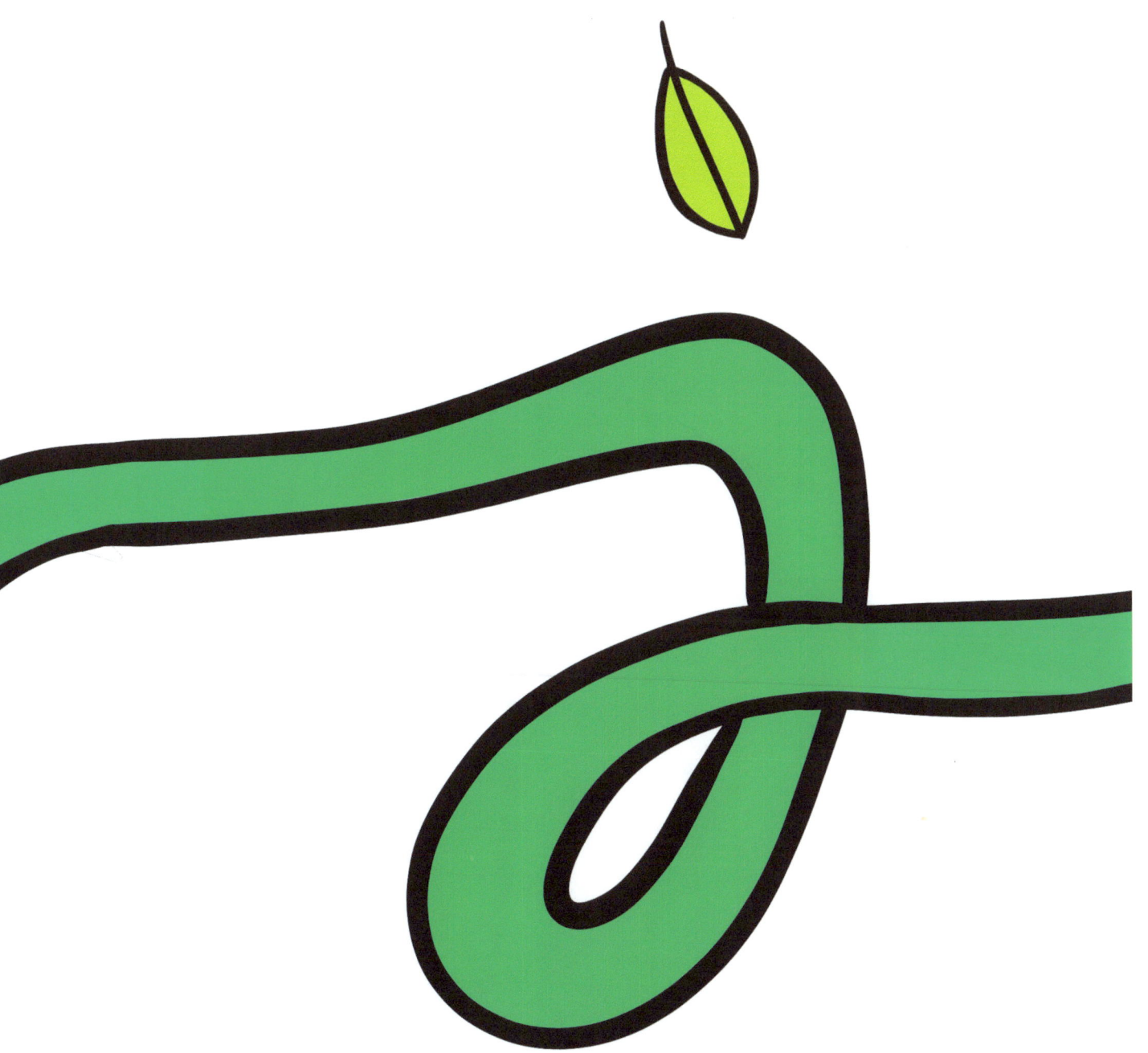

Young Picture Book Artists Program

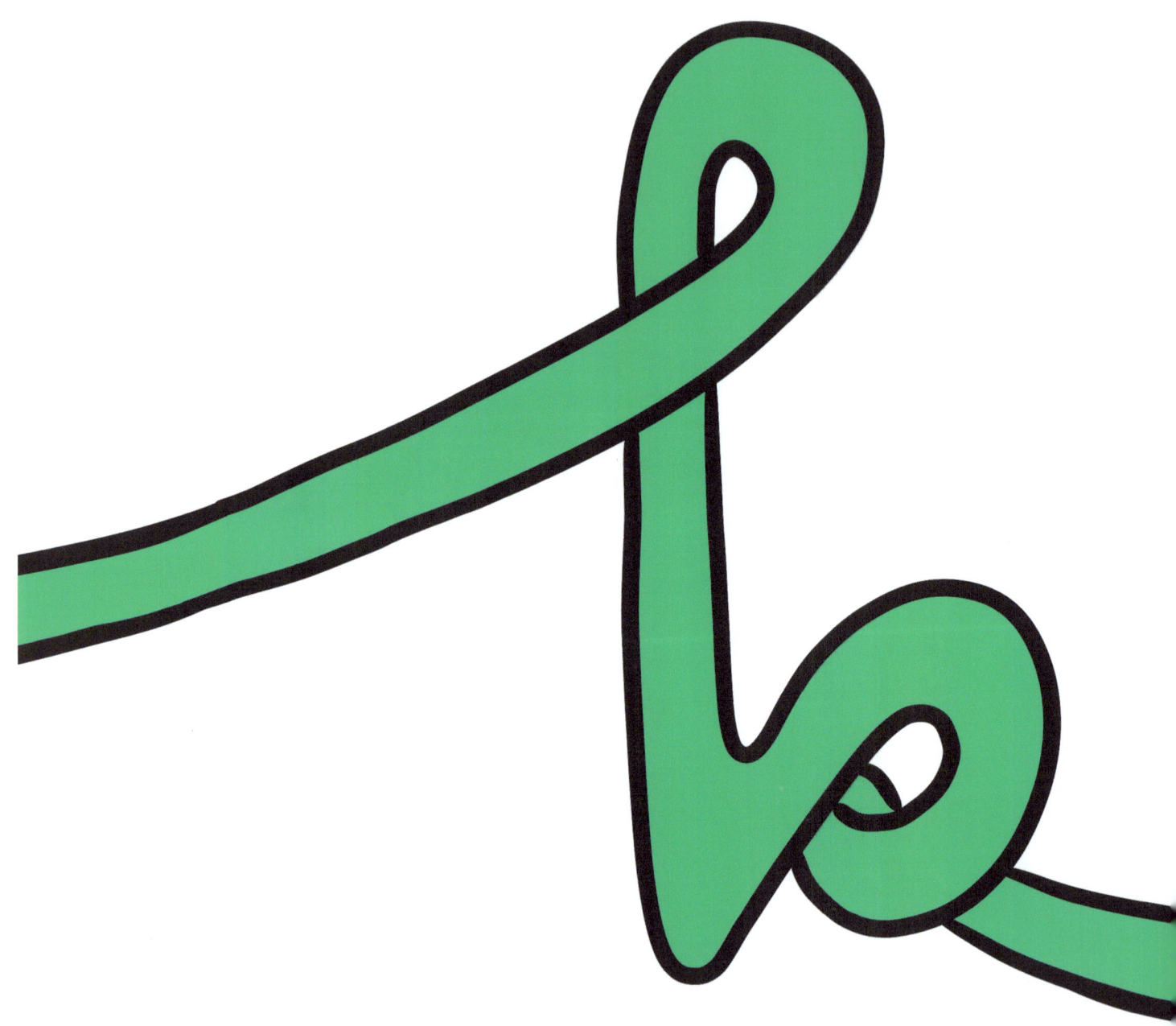

The Cursive Lettered Snake

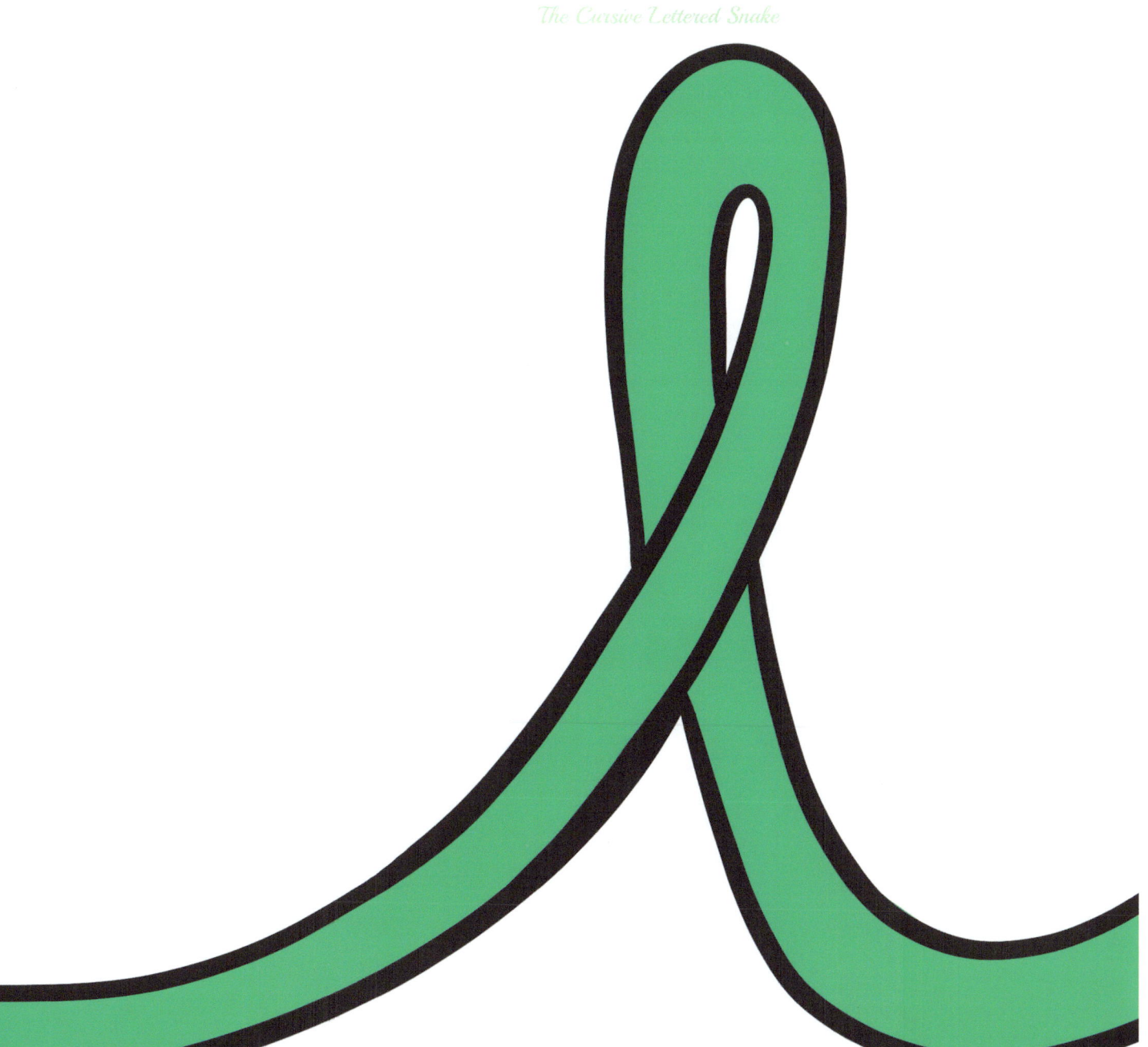

Young Picture Book Artists Program

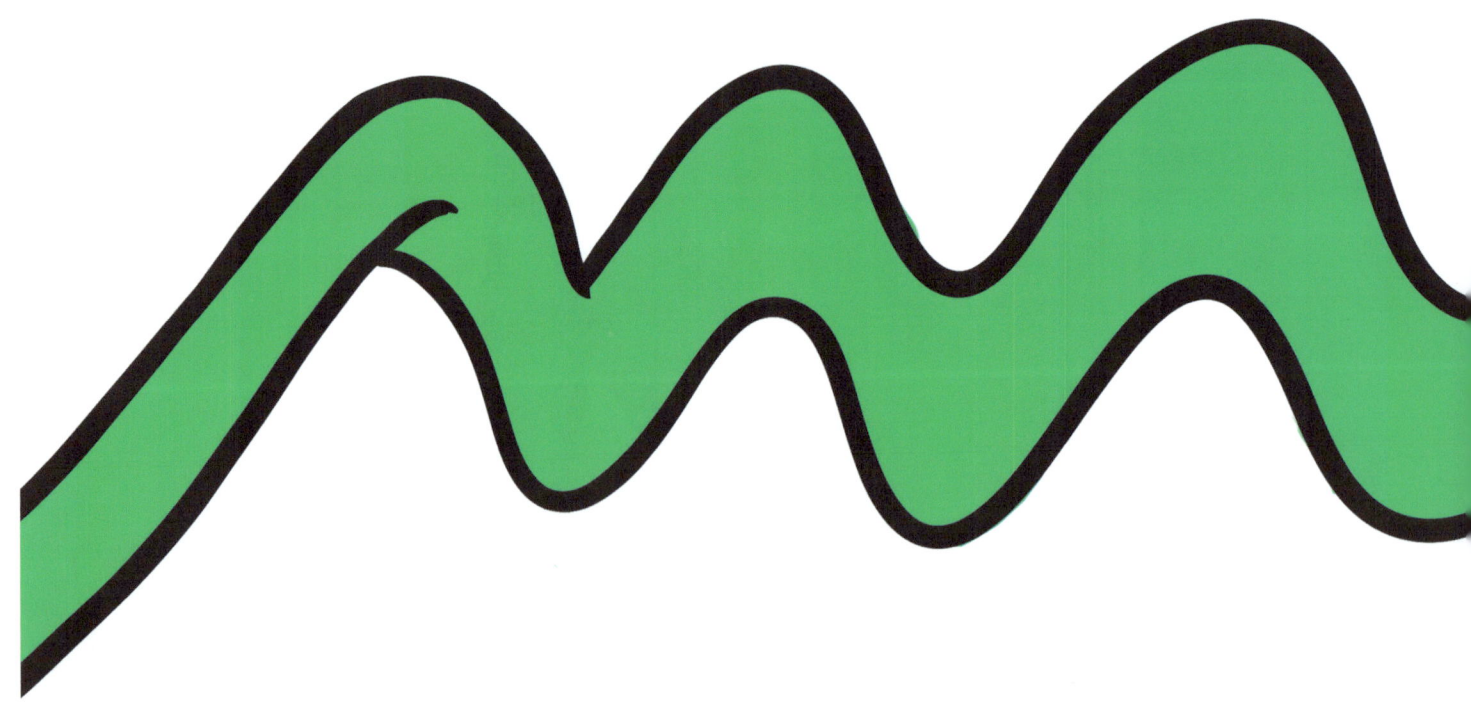

The Cursive Lettered Snake

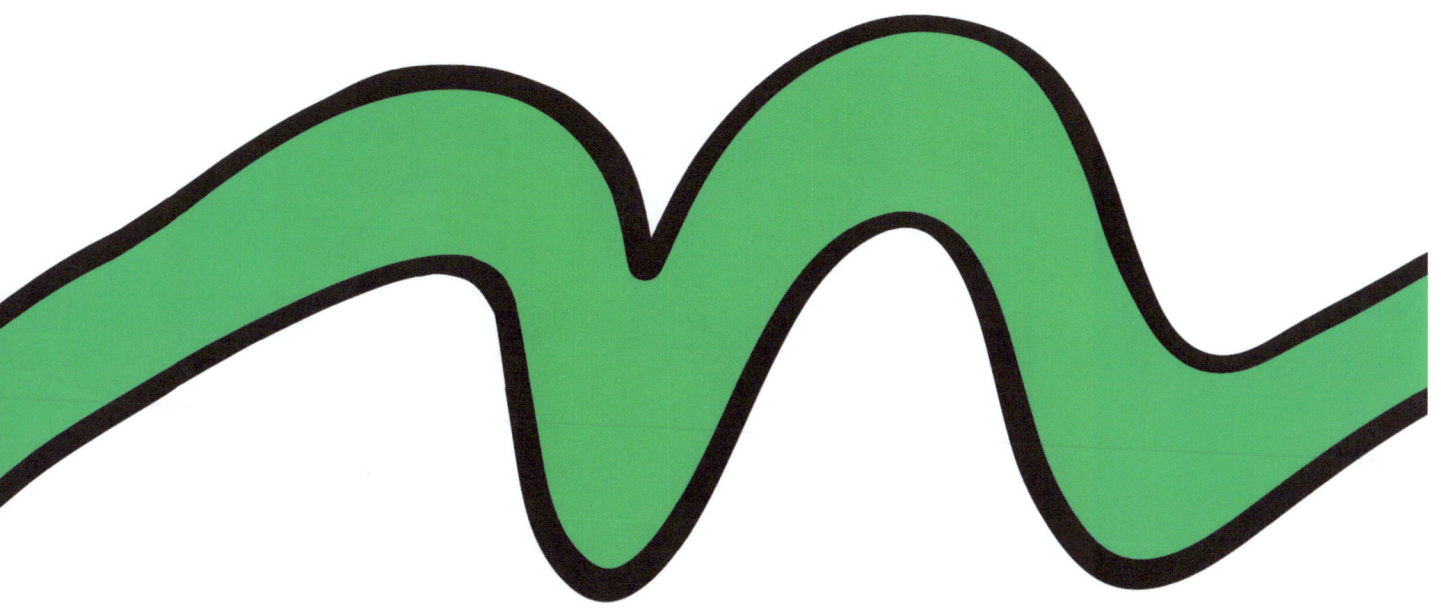

Young Picture Book Artists Program

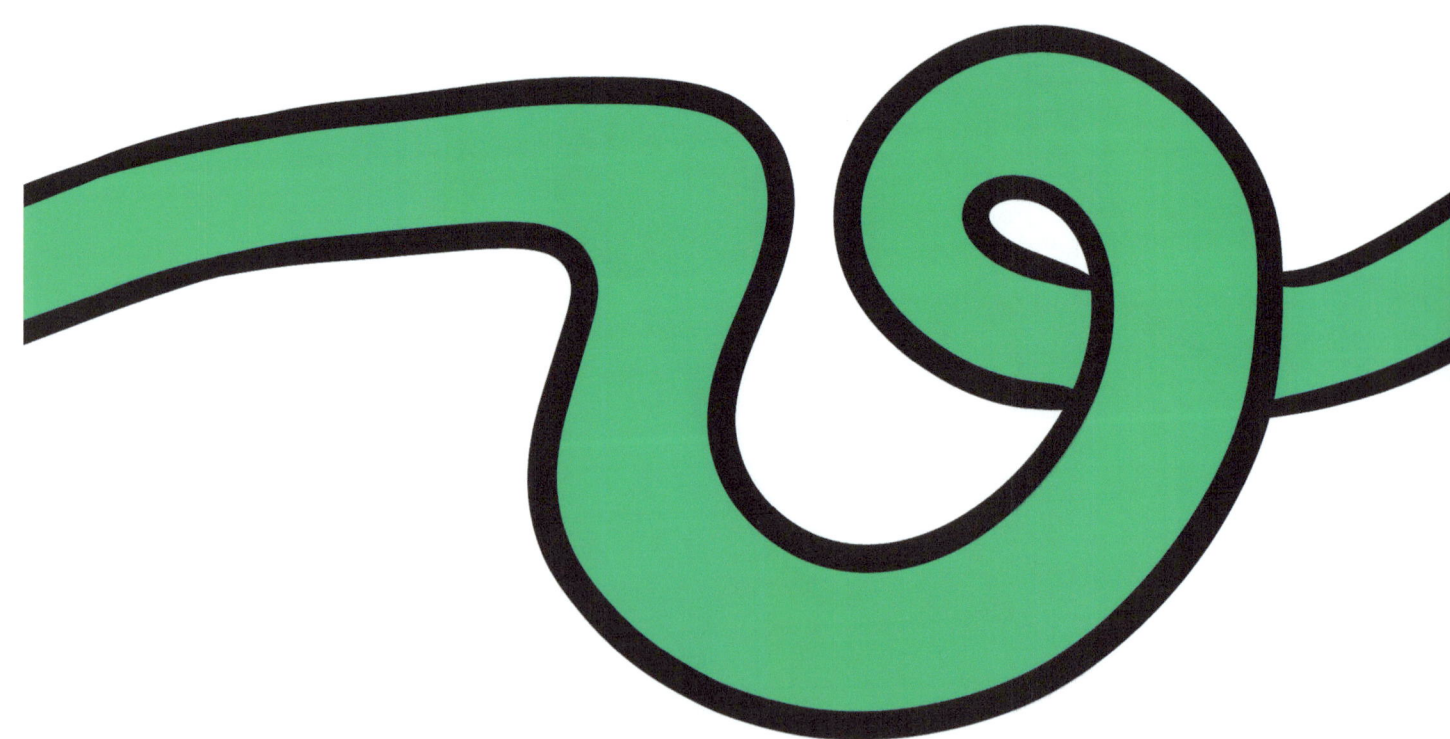

The Cursive Lettered Snake

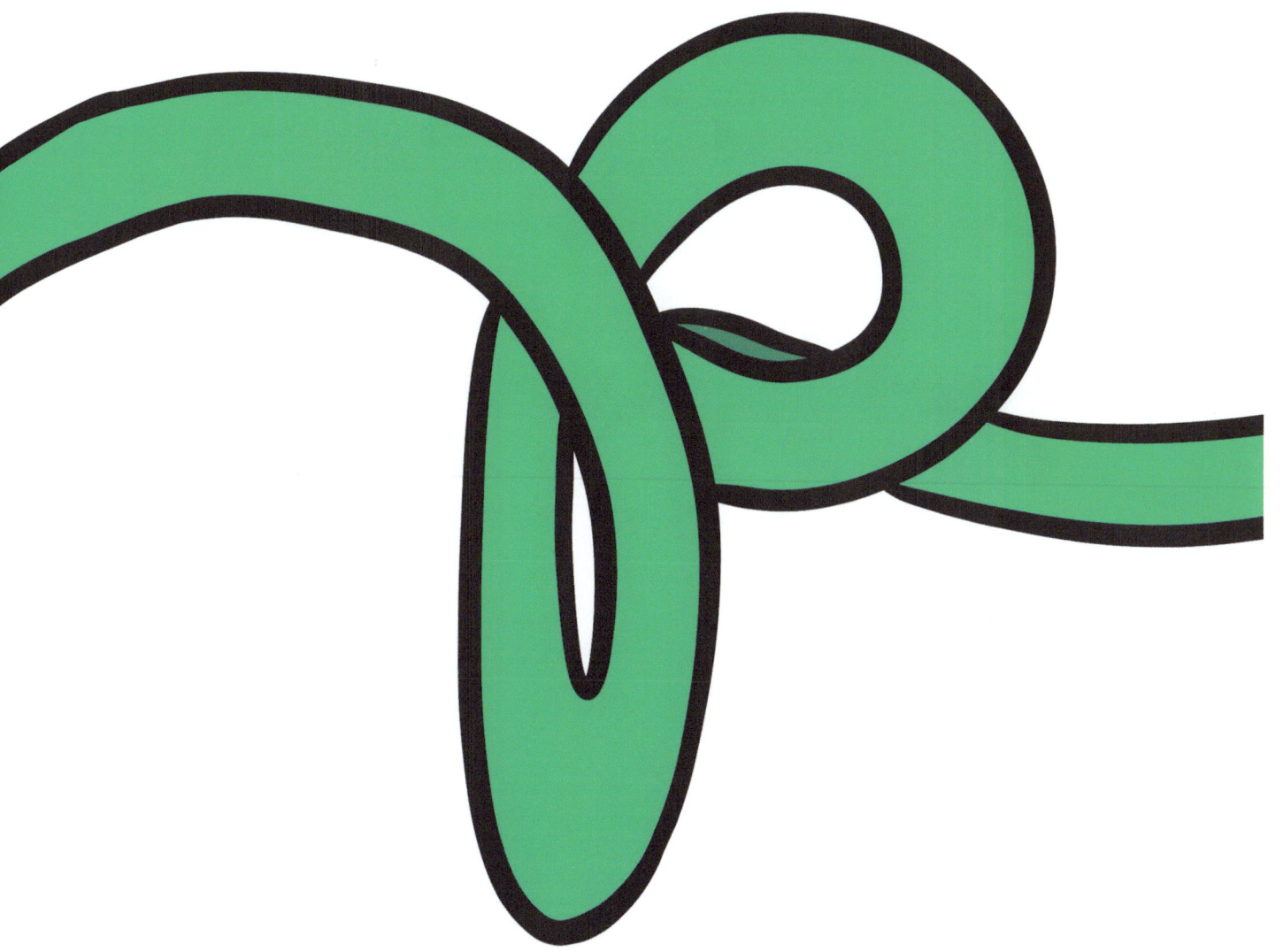

Young Picture Book Artists Program

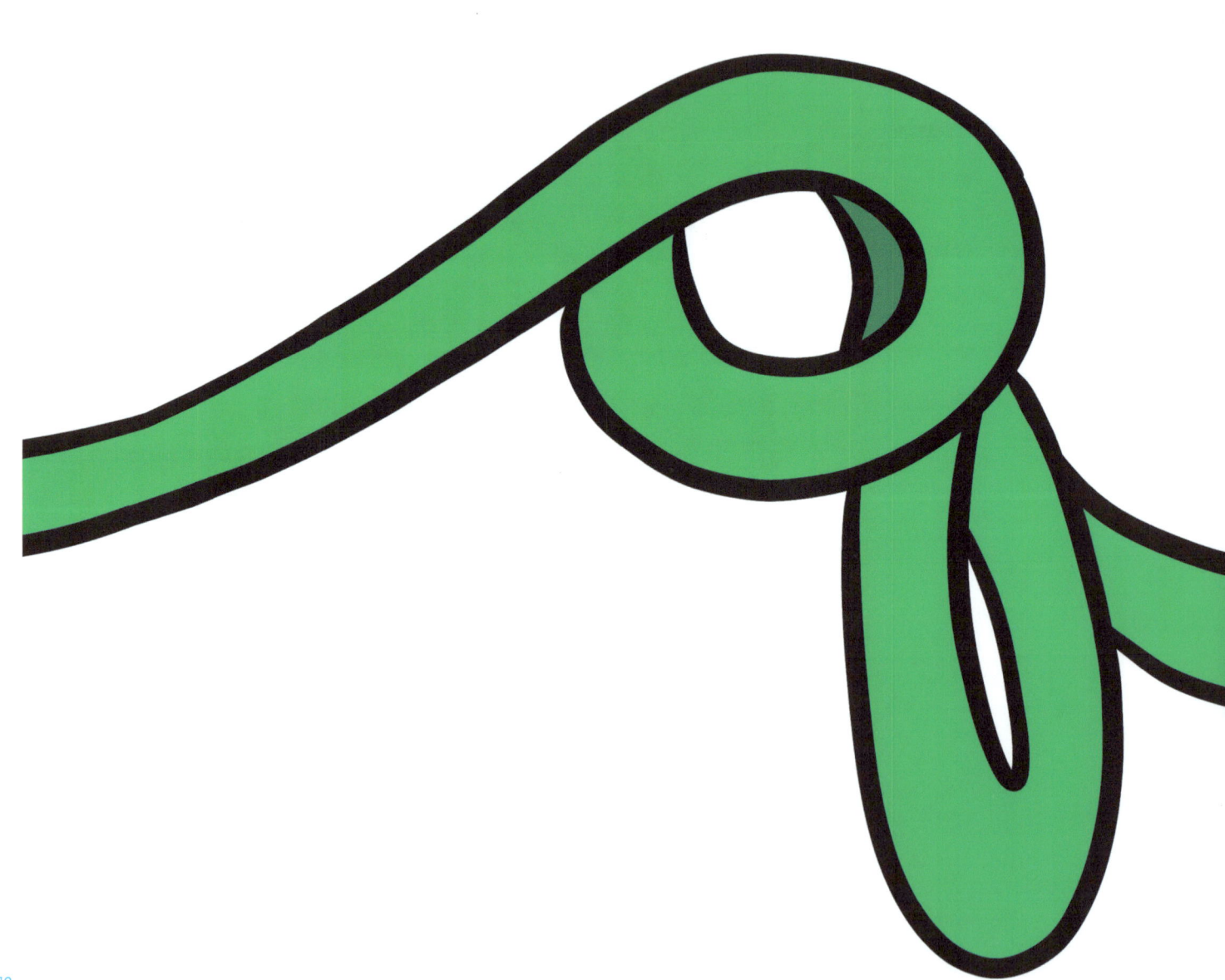

The Cursive Lettered Snake

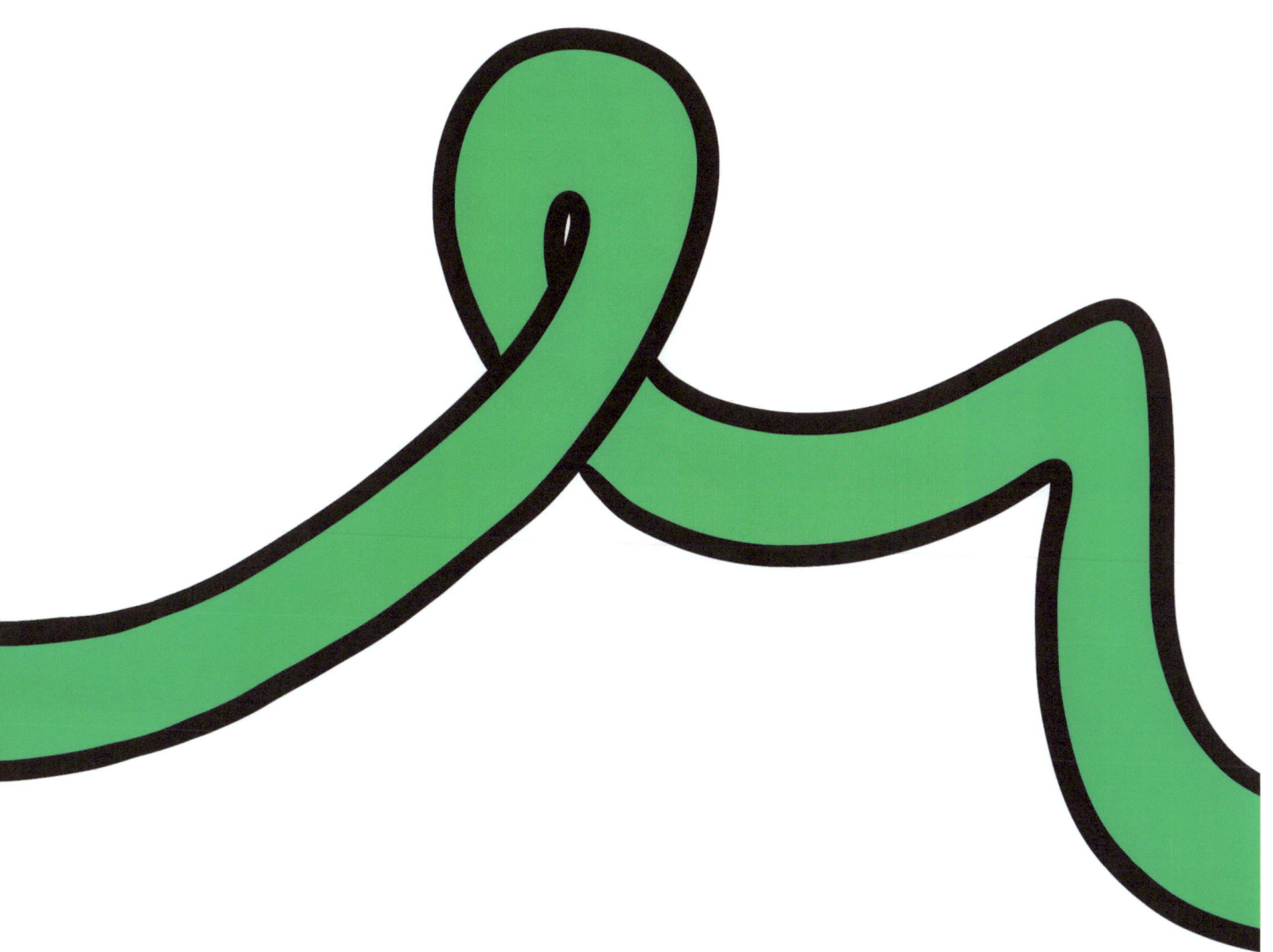

Young Picture Book Artists Program

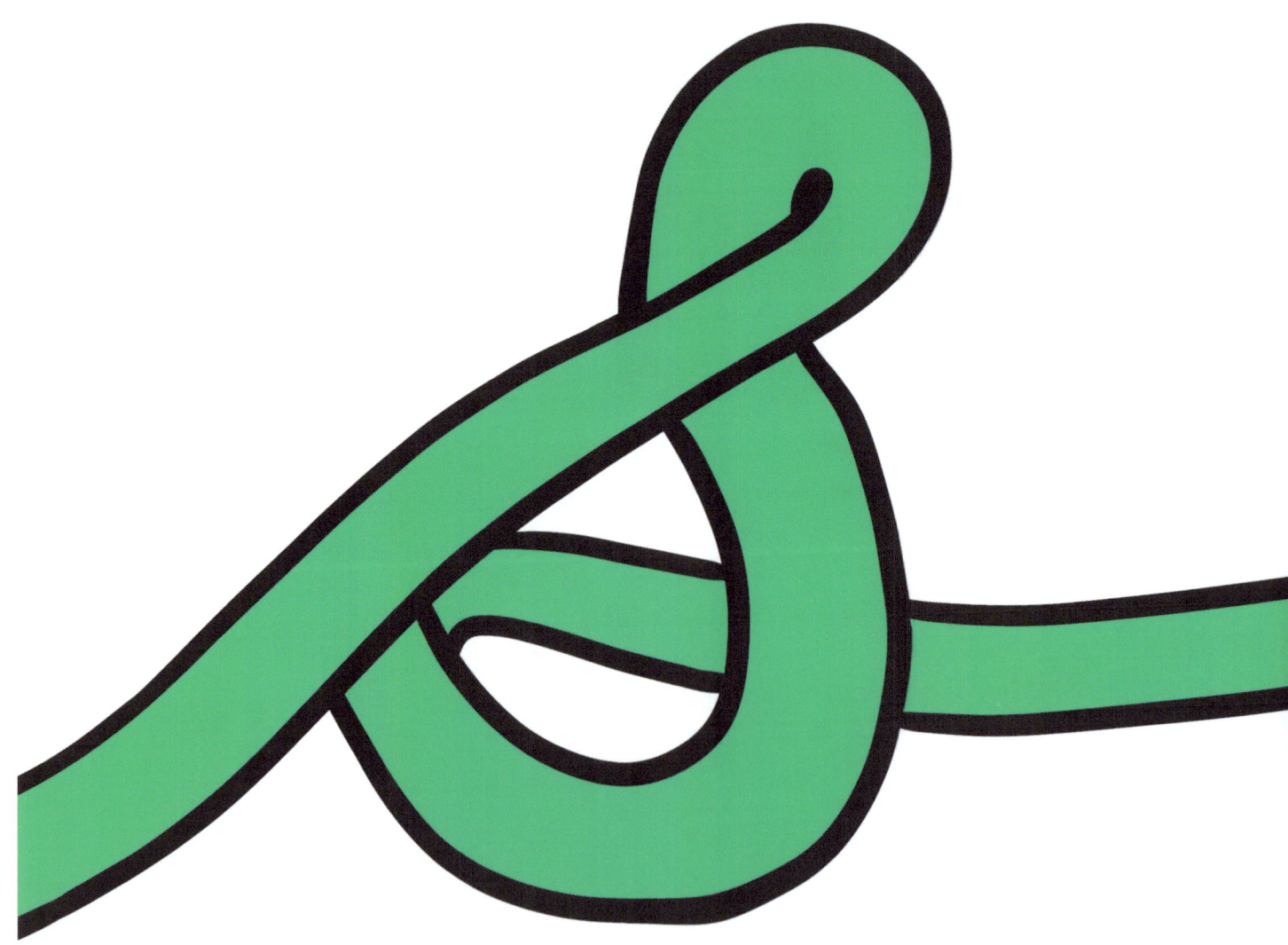

The Cursive Lettered Snake

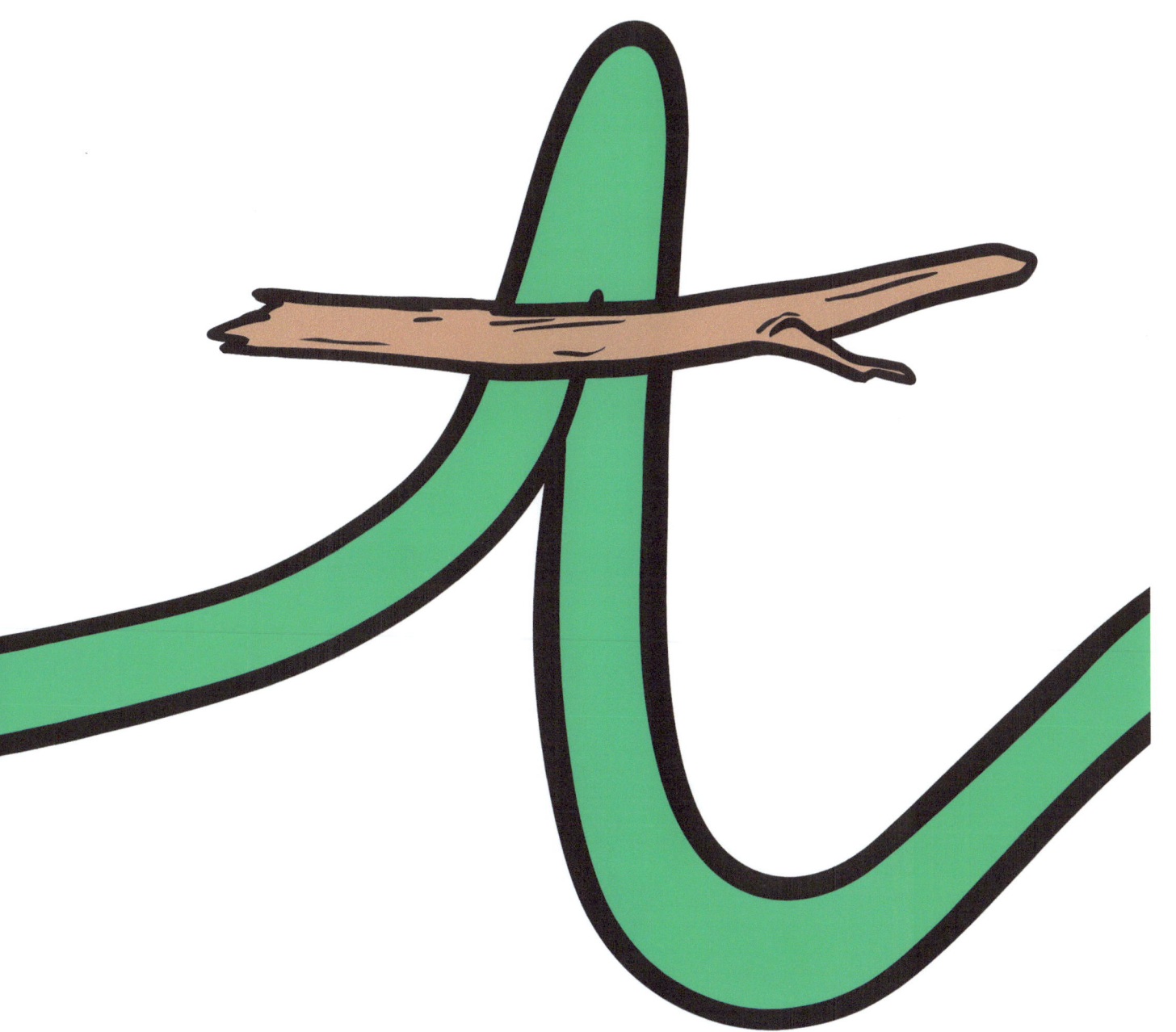

Young Picture Book Artists Program

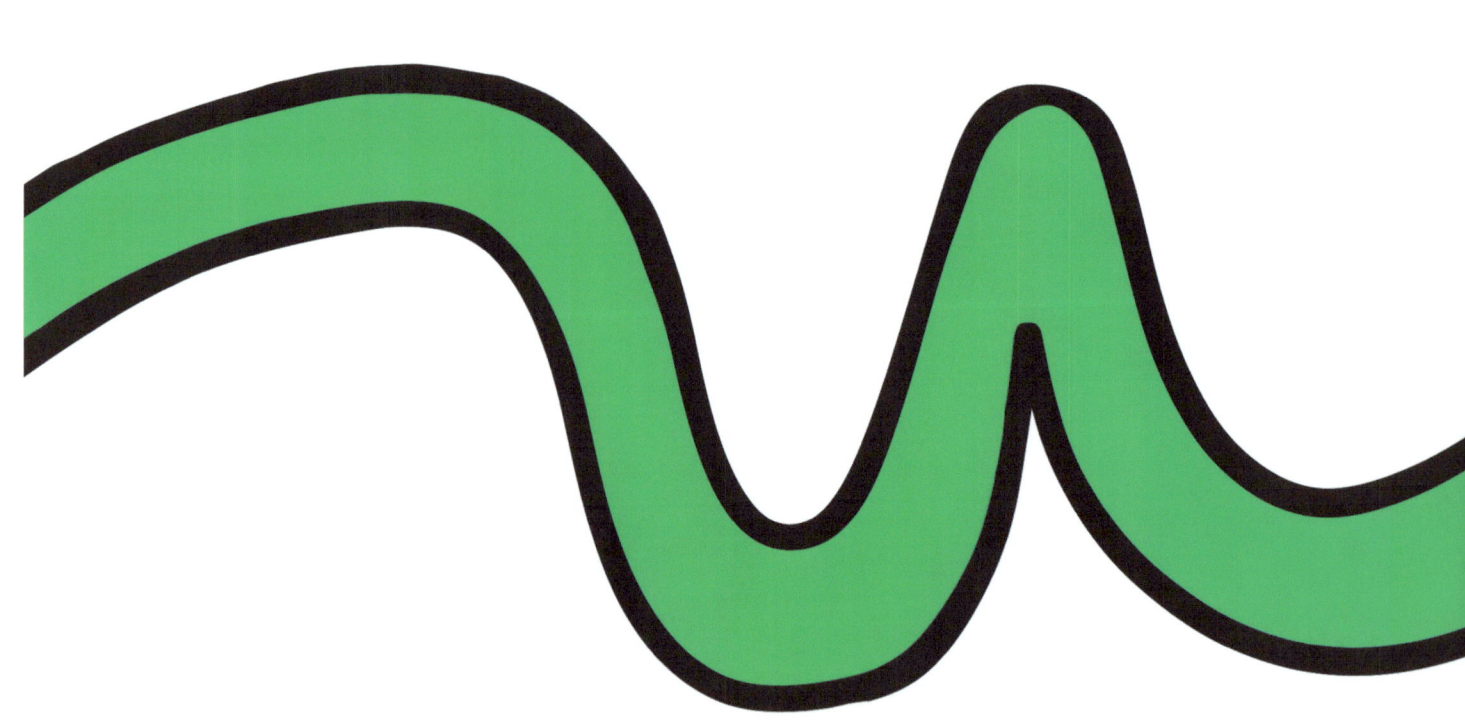

The Cursive Lettered Snake

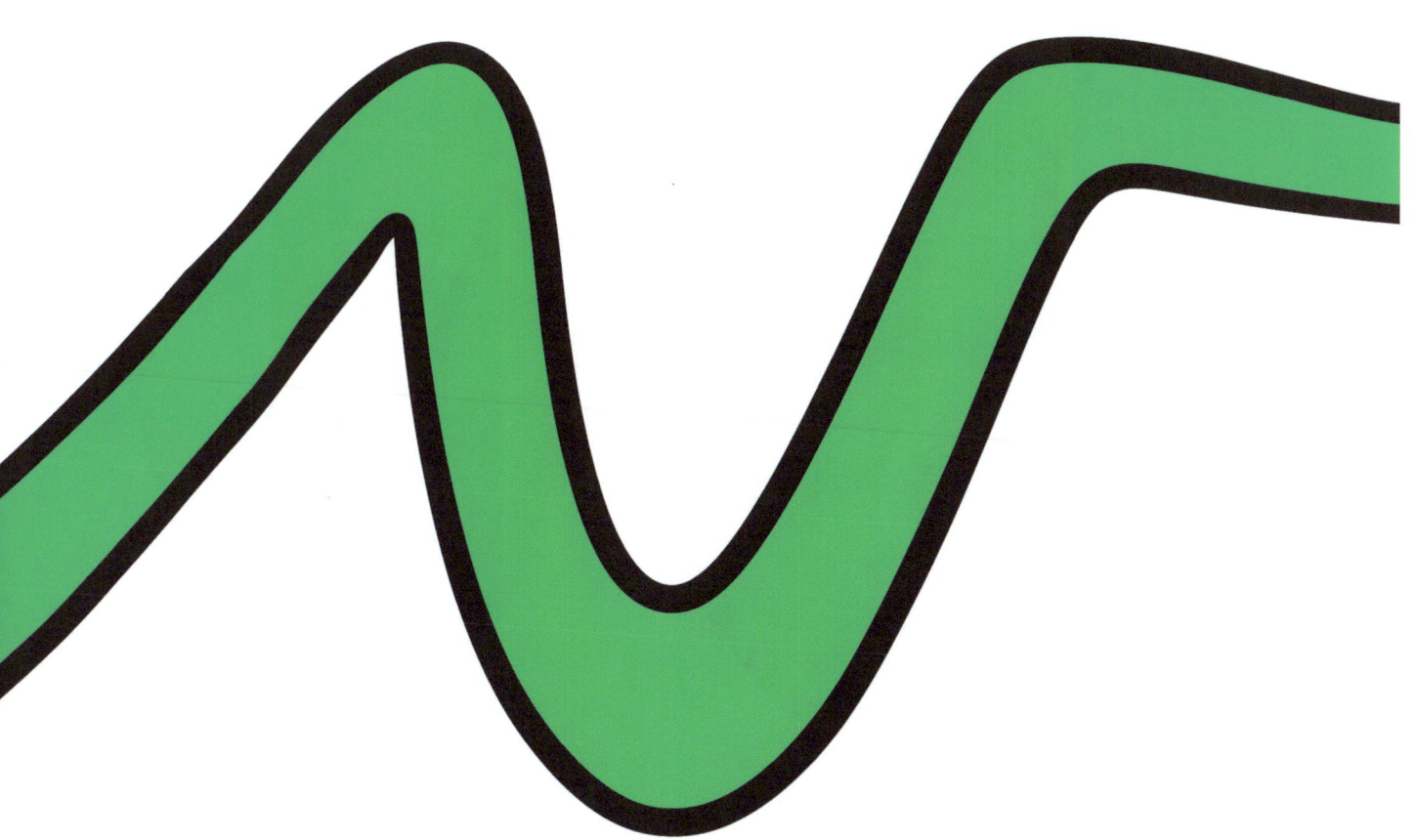

Young Picture Book Artists Program

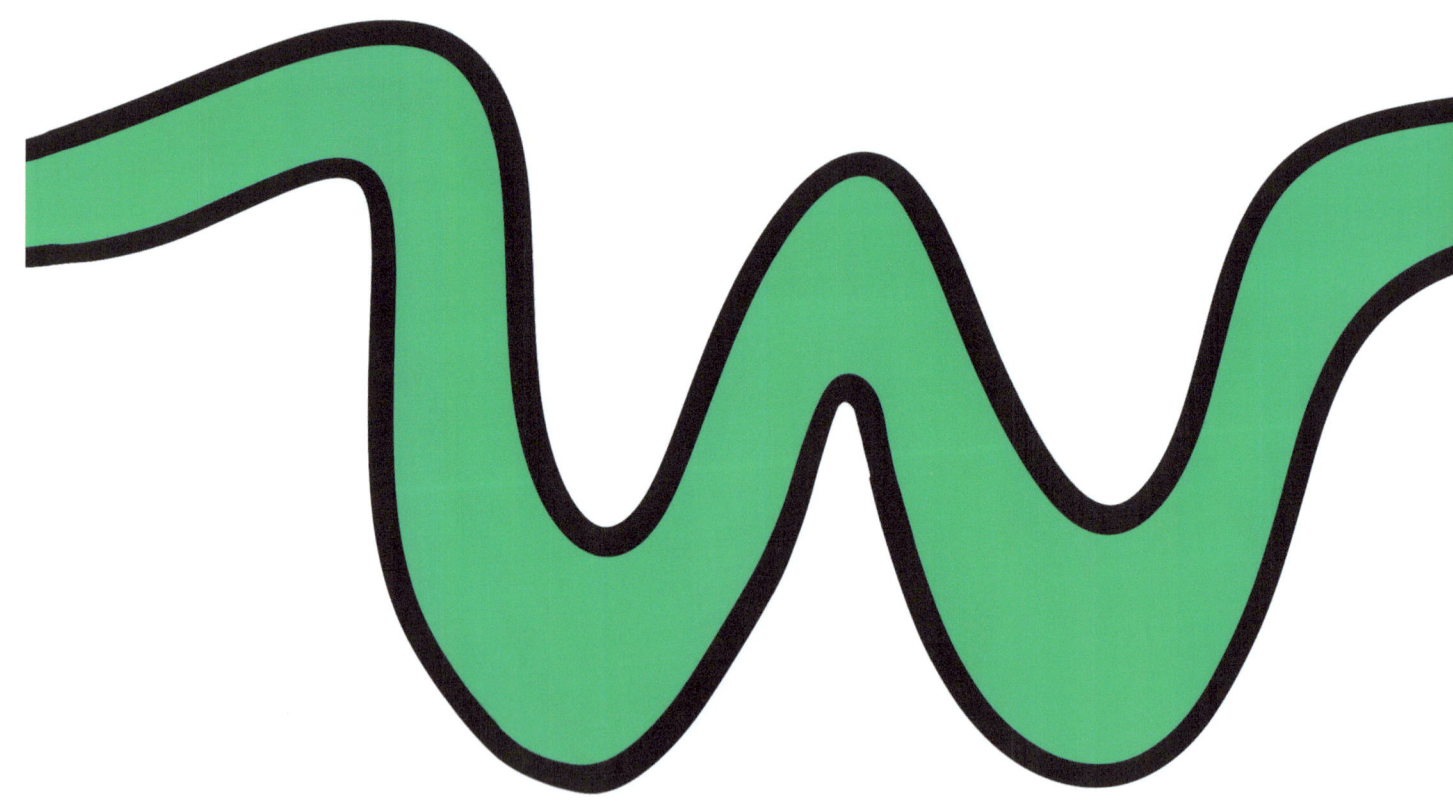

The Cursive Lettered Snake

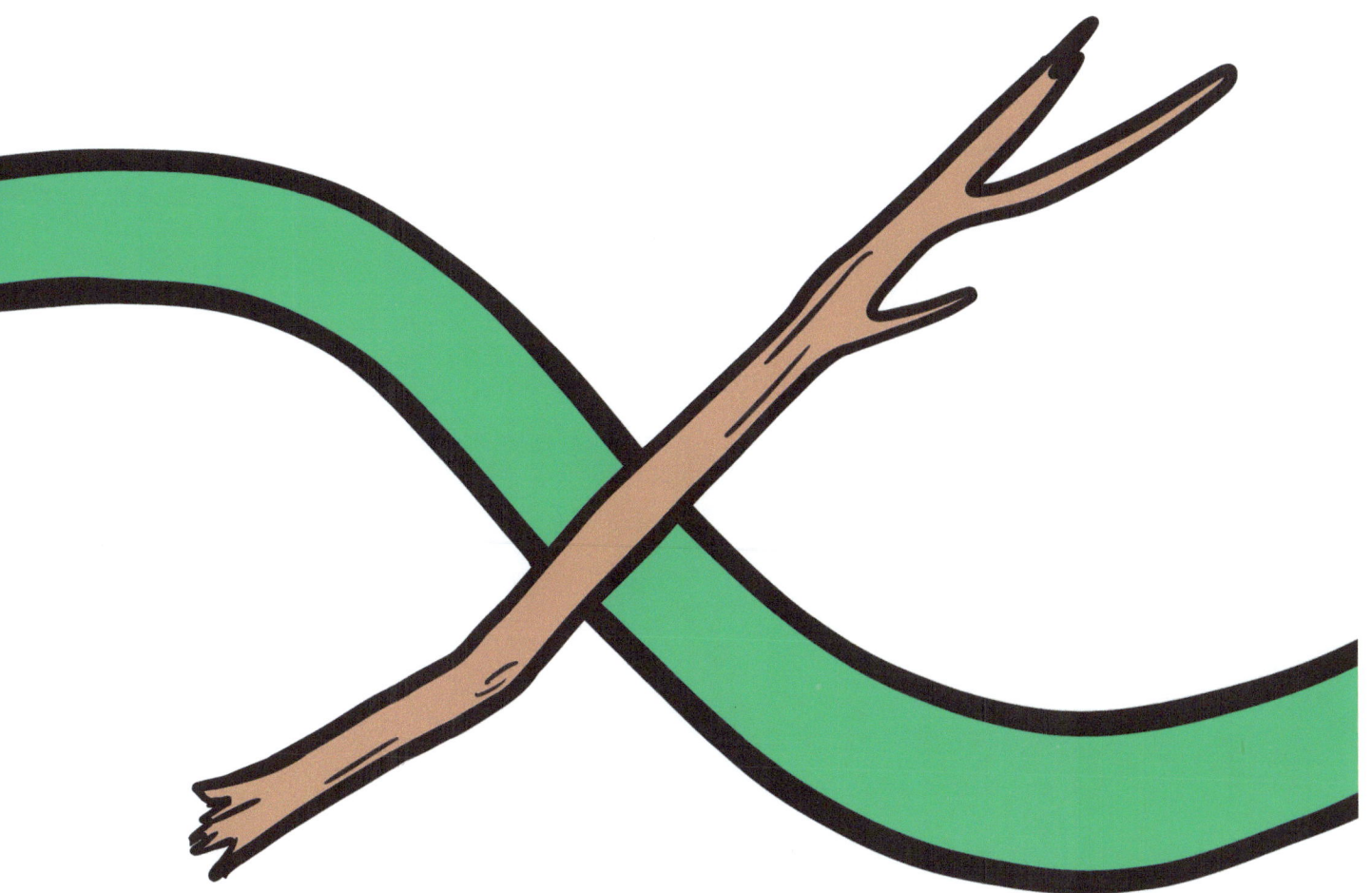

Young Picture Book Artists Program

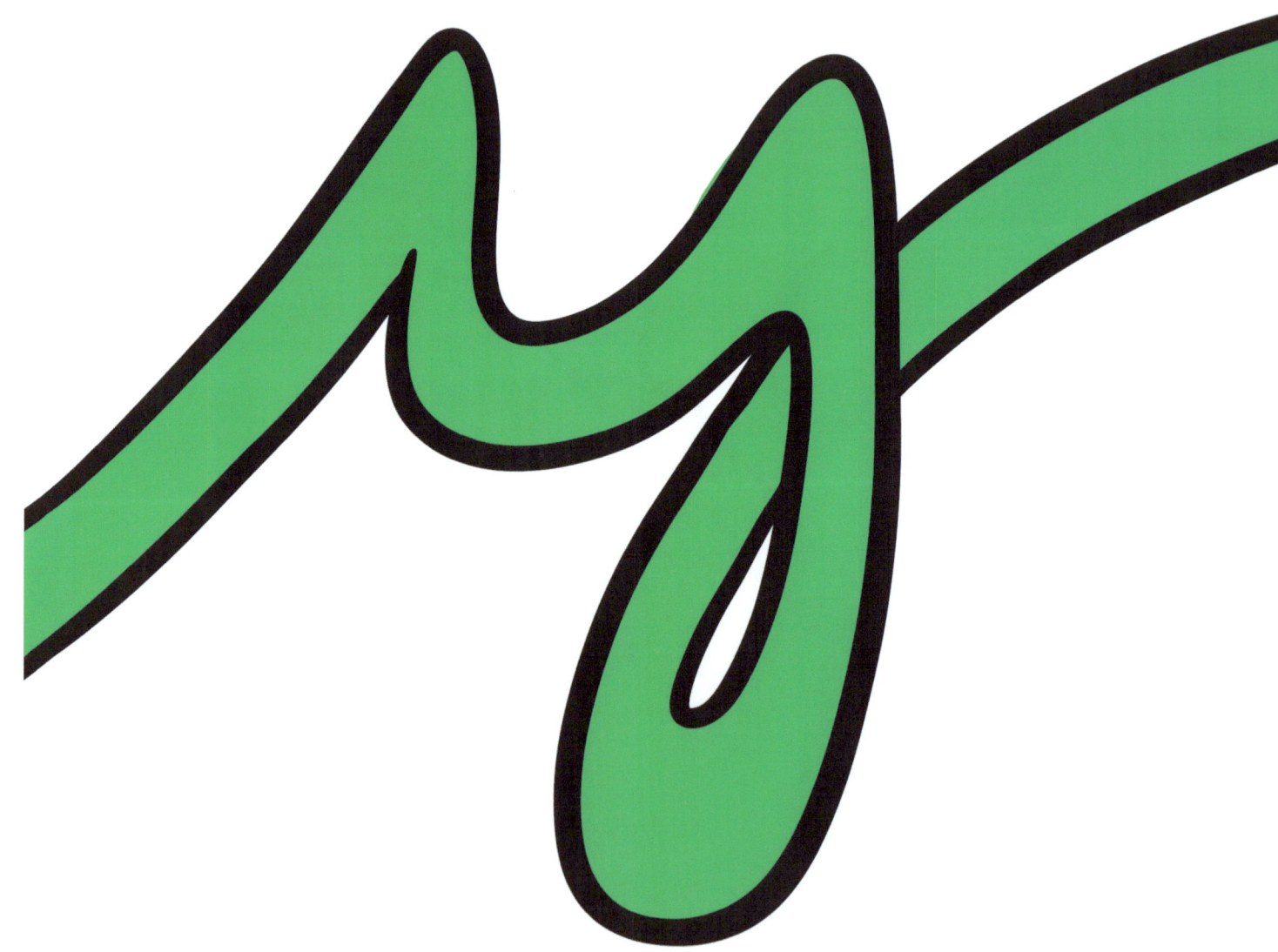

The Cursive Lettered Snake

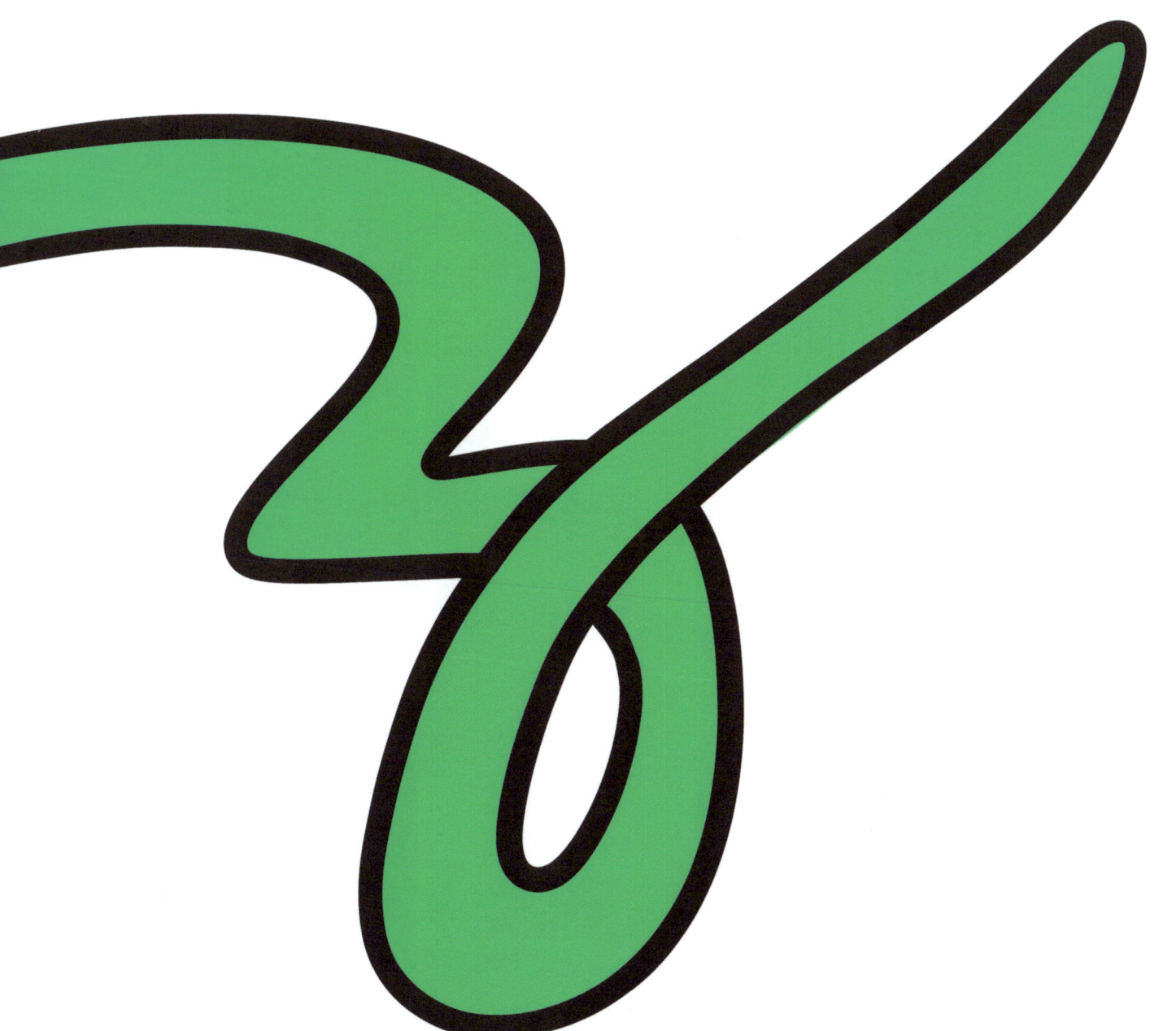

Young Picture Book Artists Program

The Cursive Lettered Snake

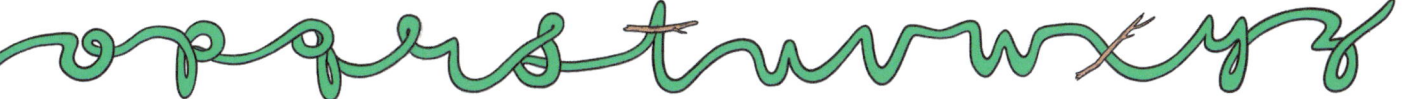

Young Picture Book Artists Program

Elaine V. Kuang

Born in 2006 in Chongqing, immigrated to the United States when she was 3 years old with her parents. She is currently studying at Ruben S. Ayala high school in Los Angeles.

PUBLISHED WORKS
Author/Editor/Cover designer/Book designer, *The Cursive Lettered Snake,* Los Angeles: Losget Press, 2022.
Author/Editor/Cover designer/Book designer, *Elaine Kuang: The Colors When Time Begins,* Los Angeles: Losget Press, 2022.
Author/Editor/Cover designer/Book designer, *A Dream,* Los Angeles: Losget Press, 2022.
Editor/Cover designer/Book designer, *Ineffable Year, Ineffable Flower,* Los Angeles: Losget Press, 2022.
Editor, *Mark Harris: East 100,* Los Angeles: Losget Press, 2022.
5 artworks were selected in *Blooming Passion: International Youth Artist Artwork Series (3)*, Los Angeles: Losget Press, 2022.
Editor/Cover designer, *Blooming Passion: International Youth Artist Artwork Series (3)*, Los Angeles: Losget Press, 2022.
5 artworks were selected in *Beaming Youth: International Youth Artist Artwork Series (2)*, Los Angeles: Losget Press, 2021.
Editor, *Beaming Youth: International Youth Artist Artwork Series (2),* Los Angeles: Losget Press, 2021.
5 artworks were selected in *The Geniuses in the Morning: International Youth Artist Artwork Series (1)*, Los Angeles: Losget Press, 2020.
Editor, *The Geniuses in the Morning: International Youth Artist Artwork Series (1)*, Los Angeles: Losget Press, 2020.
1 artwork was selected in *The Rising Young Artists From the East*, Los Angeles: Losget Press, 2019.

HONOR
Person of the Year 2021, International Society of Young Artists, USA, 2021.
Gold Award for Art, 4th Liberty Awards, International Society of Young Artists, USA, 2021.
Gold Award for Art, 3rd Liberty Awards, International Society of Young Artists, USA, 2020.
Person of the Year 2019, International Society of Young Artists, USA, 2019.
Gold Award for Art, 2nd Liberty Awards, International Society of Young Artists, USA, 2019.
Pride Award in recognition of Empathy, Magnolia Junior High, USA, 2019
Bronze Award for Art, 1st Liberty Awards, International Society of Young Artists, USA, 2018.
Principal's Award for Exceptional Performance in Collaborating and Communicating, Gerald F. Litel Elementary School, USA, 2017.
Certificate of Excellence for outstanding performance in SBAC Test, Gerald F. Litel Elementary School, USA, 2017
Honor Roll in recognition of Excellence in Scholarship, E.J. Marshall Elementary School, USA, 2015
Principal's Honor Roll in recognition of Academics, E.J. Marshall Elementary School, USA, 2014-2015.
Honor Roll in recognition of Excellence in Scholarship, E.J. Marshall Elementary School, USA, 2014
Super Citizenship Award, Washington Elementary School, USA, 2014
Principal's Honor Roll (Month of May), Washington Elementary School, USA, 2014

Principal's Honor Roll (Month of April), Washington Elementary School, USA, 2014
Principal's Honor Roll (Month of December), Washington Elementary School, USA, 2013
Principal's Honor Roll (Month of March), Washington Elementary School, USA, 2013
Super Citizenship Award, Washington Elementary School, USA, 2013
Certificate of Excellence for attaining advanced level of achievement on District-wide Mathematics Assessment, Pomona Unified School District, USA, 2012
Certificate of Excellence for attaining advanced level of achievement on District-wide Language Arts Assessments, Pomona Unified School District, USA, 2012

JOINED SOCIETIES
President of Detectives Club at Ruben S. Ayala High School, USA, since 2022.
Member of The National Society of High School Scholars, USA, since 2020.
Member/Chief Representative of Los Angeles of the International Society of Young Artists, USA, since 2019.
Member of National Junior Honor Society, USA, 2018-2019.

The Young Picture Book Artists Program Publications List

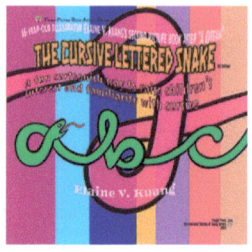

The Cursive Lettered Snake, Los Angeles: Losget Press, 2022.

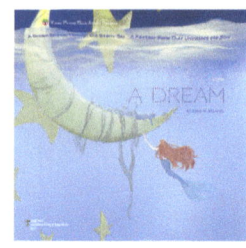

A Dream, Los Angeles: Losget Press, 2022.

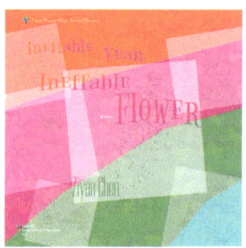

Ineffable Year, Ineffable Flower, Los Angeles: Losget Press, 2022.

The "Vibrant Future" International Education Project for Young Artists Publications List

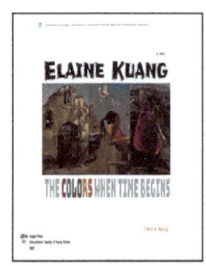

Elaine Kuang: The Colors When Time Begins, Los Angeles: Losget Press, 2022.

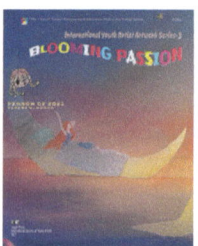

Blooming Passion: International Youth Artist Artwork Series-3, Los Angeles: Losget Press, 2022.

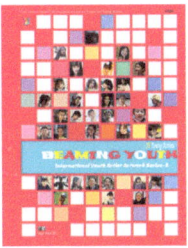

Beaming Youth: International Youth Artist Artwork Series-2, Los Angeles: Losget Press, 2021.

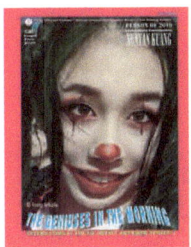

The Geniuses in the Morning: International Youth Artist Artwork Series-1, Los Angeles: Losget Press, 2020.

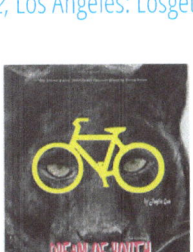

Dream of Youth, Los Angeles: Losget Press, 2019.

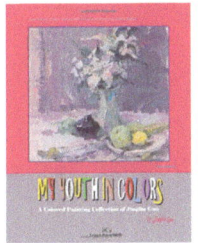

My Youth in Colors, Los Angeles: Losget Press, 2019.

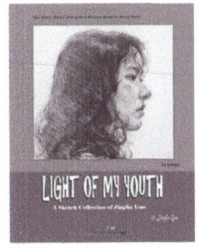

Light of My Youth. Losget Press, 2019.

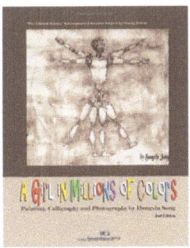

A Girl in Millions of Colors, Los Angeles: Losget Press, 2019.

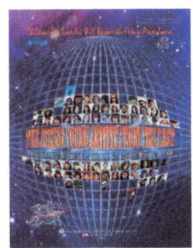

The Rising Young Artists from the East, Los Angeles: Losget Press, 2019.

Young Picture Book Artists Program

The Cursive Lettered Snake

Author: Elaine V. Kuang
Adviser: Mark Harris
Editor-in-Chief: Mark Harris
Editors: Elaine V. Kuang, Xinping Luan
Cover designer: Elaine V. Kuang
Book designer: Elaine V. Kuang

Copyright © 2022 by International Society of Young Artists
All rights reserved.
Published in the United States by Losget Press, Los Angeles.
Originally published in paperback in the United States by Losget Press, in 2022.
Library of Congress Cataloging-in-Publication Data
Names: Kuang, Elaine V., author.
Title: The Cursive Lettered Snake/ Elaine V. Kuang.
Description: First edition. | Los Angeles: Losget Press, 2022.
Identifiers: LCCN: 2022916438/ ISBN: 978-1-951364-36-6
www.isoya.org
E-mail: isoya2018@gmail.com
First printing. 2022.

www.ingramcontent.com/pod-product-compliance
Lightning Source LLC
Chambersburg PA
CBHW051153220526
45473CB00003B/765